REA: THE TEST PREP AP TEACHERS RECOMMEND

AP® PSYCHOLOGY
CRASH COURSE®

By Larry Krieger

Research & Education Association
Visit our website at: www.rea.com

Research & Education Association
61 Ethel Road West
Piscataway, New Jersey 08854
E-mail: info@rea.com

AP® PSYCHOLOGY CRASH COURSE®

Published 2017

Copyright © 2015 by Research & Education Association, Inc. Prior edition copyright © 2010 by Research & Education Association, Inc. All rights reserved. No part of this book may be reproduced in any form without permission of the publisher.

Printed in the United States of America

Library of Congress Control Number 2014944460

ISBN-13: 978-0-7386-1190-7
ISBN-10: 0-7386-1190-5

Crash Course® and REA® are registered trademarks of Research & Education Association, Inc.

AP PSYCHOLOGY CRASH COURSE TABLE OF CONTENTS

PART I:

Introduction

PART II:

Key Content Review

PART III: Key Themes and Facts

PART IV: Test-Taking Strategies

ONLINE PRACTICE EXAM........... *www.rea.com/studycenter*

ABOUT THIS BOOK

REA's *AP Psychology Crash Course* is the first book of its kind for the last-minute studier or any AP student who wants a quick refresher on the course. The *Crash Course* is based on a careful analysis of the AP Psychology Course Description outline and actual AP test questions released by the College Board.

Written by an AP teacher, our easy-to-read format gives students a crash course in the major ideas, theories, and domains in psychology. Our author has studied the topics and types of questions that have appeared most frequently on the AP Psychology exam. His targeted review chapters offer students a concise way to learn all the important AP material before the test.

Unlike other test preps, REA's *AP Psychology Crash Course* gives you a review specifically focused on what you really need to study in order to ace the exam. The introduction discusses eight keys for success and shows you strategies to help you score higher. A list of Key Terms all AP Psychology students must know is also included.

Part Two is a complete crash course in Psychology. These 14 targeted chapters focus on the subjects tested on the AP exam and cover everything from the history of psychology to treatment of abnormal behavior. Part Three offers an overview of the Key Themes and Facts you need to know for exam day.

Part Four focuses exclusively on test-taking tactics for the AP Psychology exam. The author provides expert advice on how to master both the multiple-choice and free-response sections. Each chapter gives you specific strategies for success that will help you raise your overall point score.

To check your test readiness for the AP Psychology exam, either before or after studying this *Crash Course*, take REA's **FREE online practice exam**. To access your practice exam, visit the online REA Study Center at *www.rea.com/studycenter* and follow the on-screen instructions. This true-to-format test features automatic scoring, detailed explanations of all answers, and diagnostic score reporting that will help you identify your strengths and weaknesses so you'll be ready on exam day!

Good luck on your AP Psychology exam!

ABOUT OUR AUTHOR

Larry Krieger earned a B.A. in Psychology from the University of North Carolina at Chapel Hill and an M.S. from Wake Forest University. In a career spanning more that 35 years, Mr. Krieger has taught a variety of AP subjects. His popular courses were renowned for their energetic presentations, commitment to scholarship, and helping students achieve high AP exam scores. All of Mr. Krieger's students scored above a 3 on their APs, with most students scoring a 4 or a 5. In 2004 and 2005, the College Board recognized Mr. Krieger as one of the nation's foremost AP teachers.

Mr. Krieger's success has extended far beyond the classroom. He has written several history textbooks and is a co-author of REA's *AP Art History* test preparation guide. His latest venture, the *AP Crash Course* series, helps students strategically and effectively prepare for their AP exams.

The author would like to thank his wife, Susan, for her invaluable assistance, support, and patience during the writing of this book. He also extends his thanks to Michael D'Alessio for his advice and help on Chapters 5 and 6 of this book.

ACKNOWLEDGMENTS

In addition to our author, we would like to thank Larry B. Kling, Vice President, Editorial, for his overall guidance, which brought this publication to completion; Pam Weston, Publisher, for setting the quality standards for production integrity and managing the publication to completion; and Diane Goldschmidt, Managing Editor, for editorial project management.

We also extend our special thanks to Nancy Fenton, AP Psychology teacher at Adlai E. Stevenson High School in Lincolnshire, Illinois for updating this edition and Kathy Caratozzolo of Caragraphics, for typesetting this edition.

PART I:

INTRODUCTION

Eight Keys for Success on the AP Psychology Exam

AP Psychology textbooks are very thick and contain hundreds of terms, the names of famous psychologists, and landmark research studies. If all of these facts had an equal chance of appearing on your Advanced Placement Psychology Exam, studying would be a nightmare. Where would you begin? What would you emphasize? As you prepare for this exam, is there any information you can safely omit? Or must you study everything?

1. Understanding the AP Psychology Scale

Many students believe they must make close to a perfect score to receive a 5. Nothing could be further from the truth. Each AP Psychology exam contains a total of 150 points—100 for the multiple-choice and 50 for the free-response questions. Here is the score range from the 2007 Released Exam:

Score Range	AP Grade	Miminum Percent Right
113–150	5	75 percent
93–112	4	62 percent
77–92	3	51 percent
65–76	2	43 percent
0–64	1	0–42 percent

This chart is not a misprint. As is clearly shown, you can earn a 5 by correctly answering just 75 percent of the questions, a 4 by correctly answering just 62 percent of the questions, and a 3 by correctly answering just 51 percent of the questions.

2. Understanding the AP Psychology Curriculum Outline

Many students believe that members of the AP Psychology exam development committee have the freedom to write any question they wish. This widespread belief is not true. AP Psychology test writers use a detailed curriculum outline that tells them the topics that can be tested. The curriculum outline is freely available in the *AP Psychology Course Description Booklet*. Here are the fourteen topics and the percentage of multiple-choice questions devoted to each topic:

History and Approaches	2–4 percent
Research Methods	8–10 percent
Biological Bases of Behavior	8–10 percent
Sensation and Perception	6–8 percent
States of Consciousness	2–4 percent
Learning	7–9 percent
Cognition	8–10 percent
Motivation and Emotion	6–8 percent
Developmental Psychology	7–9 percent
Personality	5–7 percent
Testing and Individual Differences	5–7 percent
Abnormal Behavior	7–9 percent
Treatment of Abnormal Behavior	5–7 percent
Social Psychology	8–10 percent

3. **Understanding the Importance of the Released Exams and the AP Central Collection of Free-Response Questions**

    The College Board has released AP Psychology exams for the years 1994, 1999, 2004, and 2007. In addition, they provided an online exam for all teachers who participated in the AP course audit. Taken together, these five exams contain 500 released multiple-choice questions. In addition, the College Board's AP Central website contains a full discussion of all the free-response questions asked from 1999 to the present.

    This *Crash Course* book is based upon a careful analysis of all the released multiple-choice and free-response questions. These questions can be used to understand the priorities and patterns of the AP Psychology test writers. It is important to understand that the test writers' top priority is to write an exam that is a valid and reliable measure of a defined body of knowledge. As a result, test questions cluster around very predictable and often-repeated topics.

4. **Understanding the Importance of Key Terms, Key Psychologists, and Key Theories**

    Key terms, key psychologists, and key theories dominate the multiple-choice questions. Approximately, two-thirds of the multiple-choice questions test your knowledge of key terms. These questions typically ask you to identify either a definition of a term or the best example of a term. These key terms are defined and illustrated in Chapters 3 through 16. In addition, Chapter 2 provides a concise glossary of key terms.

    The Course Description outline specifically identifies 62 psychologists who were major figures or key contributors in the 14 major content areas covered on the AP Psychology exam. Between 15 and 20 percent of the multiple-choice questions test your ability to identify these psychologists and their theories. Chapter 17 provides a concise summary of famous psychologists and their key theories and research findings.

5. **Understanding the Importance of Research Methodology**

   Research methodology is the single most important topic on the AP Psychology exam. Taken together, the units on Research Methods (see Chapter 4) and Testing and Individual Differences (see Chapter 13) typically generate 13–15 multiple-choice questions that test your knowledge of methodology and statistics. In addition, methodology is the single most important topic tested in the free-response questions. Ten of the eighteen exams between 1992 and 2009 contained a free-response question devoted to research methodology. Interestingly, seven of the ten research methodology questions appeared on exams given in an even year.

6. **Understanding the Overlap Between the Multiple-Choice and Free-Response Questions**

   Both the multiple-choice and the free-response questions are taken from topics covered in the Course Description Booklet's Curriculum Outline. The AP Psychology Course Description booklet contains a particularly detailed topical outline. As a result, studying for the multiple-choice questions is tantamount to studying for the free-response questions. Most students fail to grasp the significance of this point. Since the multiple-choice questions are highly predictable, so are the free-response questions. The two types of questions overlap since they both test key concepts from the same topical outline.

7. **Using Your Crash Course to Build a Winning Strategy**

   This *Crash Course* book is based on a careful analysis of the Course Description topical outline and all the released questions. Chapter 2 contains a concise glossary of the key terms you absolutely, positively have to know. Chapters 3 through 16 provide you with a detailed discussion of each content area covered on the AP Psychology Exam. Chapter 17 provides you with a digest of key figures and their research findings and theories. Chapter 18 provides you with a digest of key topics that are easily confused and frequently tested. Chapters 19 and 20 discuss test-taking strategies for the multiple-choice and free-response questions.

   If you have time, review the entire book. This is desirable, but not mandatory. The chapters can be studied in any order. Each chapter provides you with a digest of key information that is repeatedly tested. Unlike most review books, the digests are not meant to be exhaustive. Instead, they are meant to focus your attention on the vital material you must study.

Focus your attention on studying a group of topics that will generate the winning coalition of points you need to score a 4 or 5. Research methods, learning, abnormal behavior, and the treatment of abnormal behavior are particularly important building blocks for any successful coalition of points. Taken together, these topics typically generate 50 points, or almost half the points you need to score a 5.

8. How to Supplement This Crash Course

Your Crash Course contains everything you need to know to score a 4 or 5, but for this important exam you should make use of everything that can help. The College Board's website has useful information to help you prepare for the exam, including released exams and sample student essays.

Also, REA's *AP Psychology All Access*® Book + Web + Mobile study system further enhances your AP exam preparation by offering a comprehensive review book plus a suite of online assessments (topic-level quizzes, mini-tests, a full-length practice test, and e-flashcards) all designed to pinpoint your strengths and weaknesses and help focus your study for the exam. Visit *www.rea.com* to learn more.

Key Terms

I. HISTORY AND APPROACHES

1. BEHAVIORAL PERSPECTIVE

   Emerged from the pioneering work of Ivan Pavlov, John B. Watson, and B.F. Skinner. Emphasizes observable behavior that can be objectively measured.

2. HUMANISTIC PERSPECTIVE

   Emerged from the pioneering work of Carl Rogers and Abraham Maslow. Emphasizes the importance of self-esteem, free will, and choice in human behavior.

3. PSYCHOANALYTIC/PSYCHODYNAMIC PERSPECTIVE

   Emerged from the pioneering work of Sigmund Freud. Emphasizes the role of unconscious conflicts in determining behavior and personality.

4. COGNITIVE PERSPECTIVE

   Influenced by the computer revolution, the cognitive perspective compares the mind to a computer that encodes, processes, and stores information. Cognitive psychologists emphasize thinking, perceiving, and information processing.

5. BIOLOGICAL PERSPECTIVE

   Emphasizes genetics, the roles of various parts of the brain, and the structure and function of individual nerve cells.

6. EVOLUTIONARY PERSPECTIVE

   Influenced by the seminal writings of Charles Darwin. Emphasizes the role played by natural selection and adaptation in the evolution of behavior and mental processes.

II. RESEARCH METHODS

7. EXPERIMENTAL METHOD

   A carefully controlled scientific procedure involving the manipulation of variables to determine cause and effect. The experimental method enables researchers to determine cause-and-effect relationships.

8. INDEPENDENT VARIABLE

   The factor that is manipulated or controlled by the experimenter.

9. DEPENDENT VARIABLE

   The factor that is measured by the experimenter. It is affected by, and thus depends on, the independent variable.

10. EXPERIMENTAL GROUP

    Group that is exposed to the independent variable.

11. CONTROL GROUP

    Group that is exposed to all experimental conditions, except the independent variable.

12. CONFOUNDING VARIABLE

    Variables that have an unwanted influence on the outcome of an experiment. Also known as extraneous variables.

13. DOUBLE-BLIND STUDY

    A procedure in which neither the researcher nor the participant knows which group received the experimental treatment. Designed to reduce experimenter bias.

14. CASE STUDY

    An in-depth examination of a single research participant.

15. CORRELATION RESEARCH

    The researcher observes or measures two or more naturally occurring variables to find the relationship between them. In correlation research, the researcher does not directly manipulate the variables.

16. CORRELATION COEFFICIENT

    A numerical value from +1.00 to -1.00 that indicates the strength and direction of the relationship between two variables. A positive correlation indicates that the two variables move or vary in the same direction. A negative correlation indicates that the two variables move or vary in opposite directions. A zero correlation indicates that there is no relationship between the two variables.

17. MEAN

A measure of central tendency that provides the average score. Any change in the highest score in a distribution must result in a change in the mean.

18. MEDIAN

A measure of central tendency that divides a frequency distribution exactly in half.

19. MODE

A measure of central tendency that identifies the most frequently occurring score in a distribution.

20. STANDARD DEVIATION

A measure of variability that indicates the average differences between the scores and their mean.

21. NORMAL DISTRIBUTION

A bell-shaped curve, describing the spread of a characteristic throughout a population. In a normal distribution, half the scores fall at or above the mean and half the scores fall at or below the mean.

22. POSITIVELY SKEWED DISTRIBUTION

Contains a preponderance of scores on the low end of the scale. The mean will be higher than the median in a positively skewed distribution.

23. NEGATIVELY SKEWED DISTRIBUTION

Contains a preponderance of scores on the high end of the scale. The mean will be lower than the median in a negatively skewed distribution.

24. P-VALUE

The probability of concluding that a difference exists when in fact the difference does not exist. A statistically significant difference is a difference not likely due to chance. By consensus, a statistically significant difference is one that would show up only 5 percent of the time or less. The smaller the p-value the more significant the results.

III. BIOLOGICAL BASES OF BEHAVIOR

25. NEURON

A highly specialized nerve cell responsible for receiving and transmitting information in electrical and chemical forms. Neurons are the fundamental building blocks of the nervous system.

26. MYELIN SHEATH

A white, fatty covering wrapped around the axons of some neurons, which increases the rate at which nerve impulses travel along the axon.

27. ACTION POTENTIAL

A brief electrical impulse by which information is transmitted along the axon of a neuron.

28. ALL-OR-NOTHING LAW

The principle that either a neuron is sufficiently stimulated and an action potential occurs or a neuron is not sufficiently stimulated and an action potential does not occur.

29. ENDORPHINS

Chemical substances in the nervous system that reduce the perception of pain.

30. NEUROTRANSMITTERS

Chemical transmitters manufactured by a neuron. For example, acetylcholine is associated with Alzheimer's disease, dopamine is linked to schizophrenia, and serotonin is related to depression.

31. SYMPATHETIC NERVOUS SYSTEM

Branch of the automatic nervous system that produces rapid physical arousal in response to perceived emergencies or threats.

32. PARASYMPATHETIC NERVOUS SYSTEM

Branch of the autonomic nervous system that calms the body, maintains bodily functions, and conserves energy.

33. HYPOTHALAMUS

Small brain structure beneath the thalamus that helps govern the release of hormones by the pituitary gland and regulates drives such as hunger and thirst.

34. **CEREBRAL CORTEX**

    A thin surface layer on the cerebral hemispheres that regulates most complex behavior, including sensations, motor control, and higher mental processes such as decision making.

35. **CEREBRAL HEMISPHERES**

    The nearly symmetrical left and right halves of the cerebral cortex. The left hemisphere specializes in verbal and analytical functions. The right hemisphere focuses on nonverbal abilities such as art and music and visual recognition tasks.

36. **CORPUS CALLOSUM**

    The bundle of nerve fibers connecting the brain's left and right hemispheres. In a procedure known as split-brain surgery, neurosurgeons cut the corpus callosum to prevent the spread of epileptic seizures by disrupting communication between the right and left hemispheres.

37. **AMYGDALA**

    An almond-shaped part of the limbic system linked to the regulation of emotional responses, especially fear.

38. **HIPPOCAMPUS**

    A curved forebrain structure that is part of the limbic system and is involved in learning and forming new memories.

IV. SENSATION AND PERCEPTION

39. **ABSOLUTE THRESHOLD**

    The minimum intensity at which a stimulus can be detected at least 50 percent of the time. For example, humans can barely detect a candle flame from 30 miles away on a clear, dark night.

40. **SENSORY ADAPTATION**

    The decline in sensitivity to a constant stimulus. For example, the longer an individual is exposed to a strong odor, the less aware of the odor the individual becomes.

41. **TRANSDUCTION**

The process by which sensory receptors convert the incoming physical energy of stimuli, such as light waves, into neural impulses that the brain can understand.

42. **SIGNAL DETECTION THEORY**

States that sensation depends on the characteristics of the stimulus, the background stimulation, and the detector. Selective attention enables you to filter out and focus on only selected sensory messages. For example, while practicing your piano you may not hear your cell phone ring. However, if you are expecting an important call, you will hear the cell phone ring.

43. **GATE-CONTROL THEORY**

Theory that explains how the nervous system blocks or allows pain signals to pass to the brain.

44. **RODS**

The long, thin visual receptor cells in the retina that are highly sensitive to light, but not to color. The rods are primarily responsible for peripheral vision and black-and-white vision. Cats have better night vision than humans because they have a higher proportion of rods to cones.

45. **CONES**

The short, thick visual receptor cells, concentrated near the center of the retina, responsible for color vision and fine detail. People who are color blind typically have deficiencies in their cones.

46. **BLIND-SPOT**

The point at the back of the retina where the optic nerve leaves the eye. Since there are no visual receptor cells, this creates a small gap in field vision called the "blind spot."

47. **COCHLEA**

The coiled, snail-shaped structure in the inner ear containing receptors for hearing.

V. STATES OF CONSCIOUSNESS

48. CIRCADIAN RHYTHM

    Biological processes that systematically vary over a period of about 24 hours. For example, the sleep-wake cycle, blood pressure, and pulse rate all follow circadian rhythms.

49. REM SLEEP

    Type of sleep during which rapid eye movements (REM) and dreams usually occur. REM sleep is often referred to as paradoxical sleep because it is simultaneously characterized by active eye movements and loss of muscle movement. The REM portion of the sleep cycle is longest during infancy.

50. HYPNOSIS

    A trancelike state of heightened suggestibility, deep relaxation, and intense focus. Hypnosis can be used to treat pain.

51. DISSOCIATION

    The splitting of consciousness into two or more simultaneous streams of mental activity.

VI. LEARNING

52. CLASSICAL CONDITIONING

    Based upon the pioneering work of Ivan Pavlov. The learning process that occurs when a previously neutral stimulus (a ringing bell) is repeatedly paired with an unconditioned stimulus (food) to elicit a conditioned response (salivation).

53. UNCONDITIONED STIMULUS

    A natural stimulus (food) that reflexively elicits a response (salivation) without the need for prior learning.

54. UNCONDITIONED RESPONSE

    An unlearned response (salivation) that is elicited by an unconditioned stimulus (food).

55. NEUTRAL STIMULUS

A stimulus (ringing bell) that produces no conditioned response prior to learning.

56. CONDITIONED STIMULUS

The conditioned stimulus was originally the neutral stimulus. When systematically paired with the unconditioned stimulus (food), the neutral stimulus (the ringing bell) becomes a conditioned stimulus as it gains the power to cause a response.

57. CONDITIONED RESPONSE

A conditioned response is a learned response elicited by the conditioned stimulus.

58. EXTINCTION

The gradual weakening of a conditioned behavior when the conditioned stimulus is repeatedly presented without the unconditioned stimulus.

59. STIMULUS GENERALIZATION

Occurs when stimuli that are similar to the original stimulus also elicit the conditioned response. For example, a three-year-old child is frightened by a white rabbit. A few days later, the same child sees a white fur coat and becomes frightened.

60. STIMULUS DISCRIMINATION

The ability to distinguish between two similar stimuli. For example, a person who is fearful of poison oak leaves, but not oak tree leaves, is exhibiting stimulus discrimination.

61. OPERANT CONDITIONING

A learning process in which behavior is shaped and maintained by consequences (rewards or punishments) that follow a response. In contrast, in classical conditioning behavior is controlled by the stimuli that precede a response.

62. REINFORCEMENT

Reinforcement strengthens a response and makes it more likely to occur.

63. POSITIVE REINFORCEMENT

A situation in which a behavior or response is followed by the addition of a reinforcing stimulus. The stimulus increases the probability that the response will occur again.

64. NEGATIVE REINFORCEMENT

A situation in which a behavior or response is followed by the removal of an aversive stimulus. Negative reinforcement increases the likelihood of a behavior by enabling a person to either escape an existing aversive stimulus or avoid an aversive stimulus before it occurs.

65. PREMACK PRINCIPLE

States that the opportunity to engage in a preferred activity can be used to reinforce a less-preferred activity.

66. CONTINUOUS REINFORCEMENT

A reinforcement schedule in which all correct responses are reinforced.

67. SHAPING

The technique of strengthening behavior by reinforcing successive approximations of a behavior until the entire correct routine is displayed.

68. INTERMITTENT REINFORCEMENT

The rewarding of some, but not all, correct responses.

69. FIXED RATIO SCHEDULE

Reinforcement occurs after a predetermined set of responses. For example, you are paid for every two lawns you mow.

70. VARIABLE RATIO SCHEDULE

Reinforcement is unpredictable because the ratio varies. For example, casino slot machines use a variable ratio schedule.

71. FIXED INTERVAL SCHEDULE

Reinforcement occurs after a predetermined time has elapsed. For example, you receive a paycheck every Friday.

72. VARIABLE INTERVAL SCHEDULE

Reinforcement occurs unpredictably since the time interval varies. For example, your teacher gives unannounced pop quizzes.

73. PUNISHMENT

Punishment is a process in which a behavior is followed by an aversive consequence that decreases the likelihood of the behavior being repeated.

74. POSITIVE PUNISHMENT

Adding an aversive stimulus that weakens a response and makes it less likely to recur.

75. NEGATIVE PUNISHMENT

Taking away a stimulus that weakens a response and makes it less likely to recur.

76. OBSERVATIONAL LEARNING

Occurs by watching others and then imitating or modeling the observed behavior.

VII. COGNITION

77. RECALL

The use of a general cue to retrieve a memory. For example, your psychology teacher asks you to write down everything you learned in last week's lesson on operant conditioning.

78. RECOGNITION

The use of a specific cue to retrieve a memory. For example, your psychology teacher asks you to answer a multiple-choice question about negative reinforcement.

79. SERIAL-POSITION EFFECT

Information at the beginning and end of a list is remembered better than material in the middle.

80. EPISODIC MEMORY

A subdivision of declarative memory that stores memories of personal experiences and events. For example, your first piano recital, first prom, and first varsity soccer goal are all episodic memories.

81. PROACTIVE INTERFERENCE

Occurs when old information interferes with recalling new information. For example, your old locker combination interferes with remembering your new locker combination.

82. RETROACTIVE INTERFERENCE

Occurs when new information interferes with recalling old information. For example, learning how to write an SAT essay interferes with the information you previously learned about how to write an ACT essay.

83. RETROGRADE AMNESIA

People who suffer from retrograde amnesia are unable to remember some or all of their past.

84. ANTEROGRADE AMNESIA

People who suffer from anterograde amnesia are unable to form new memories.

85. METHOD OF LOCI

The process of remembering several pieces of information by mentally associating an image of each with a different location.

86. PHONEMES

The smallest distinctive sound used in a language. For example, the *t* in *tardy* and the *ng* in *sing* are both phonemes.

87. MORPHEMES

The smallest units of meaning in a language. For example, the word *untouchable* consists of three morphemes—the prefix *un*, the root word *touch*, and the suffix *able*.

88. ALGORITHM

A logical, step-by-step procedure that, if followed correctly, will eventually solve a specific problem.

89. FUNCTIONAL FIXEDNESS

The tendency to think of an object as functioning only in its usual or customary way. As a result, individuals often do not see unusual or innovative uses of familiar objects.

90. CONFIRMATION BIAS

A preference for information that confirms preexisting positions or beliefs, while ignoring or discovering contradictory evidence.

91. HEURISTIC

A general rule of thumb or shortcut that is used to reduce the number of possible solutions.

92. AVAILABILITY HEURISTIC

Judging the likelihood of an event based on readily available personal experiences or news reports. For example, news of a plane crash causes a family to cancel their plane reservation and drive 750 miles in their car instead.

93. REPRESENTATIVE HEURISTIC

Judging the likelihood of an event based on how well it matches a typical example or prototype. For example, if Jake is 6 feet 4 inches tall and weighs 290 pounds, we may guess that he is an NFL lineman instead of a stockbroker.

94. DIVERGENT THINKING

A type of thinking in which problem solvers devise a number of possible alternative approaches. Divergent thinking is a major element in creativity.

VIII. MOTIVATION AND EMOTION

95. YERKES-DODSON LAW

An optimal level of psychological arousal helps performances. When arousal is too low, our minds wander and we become bored. When arousal is too high, we become too anxious and "freeze-up." People are thus motivated to seek a moderate level of stimulation that is neither too easy nor too hard.

96. HIEARARCHY OF NEEDS

Maslow's theory that lower motives (such as physiological and safety needs) must be met before advancing to higher needs (such as esteem and self-actualization).

97. ACHIEVEMENT MOTIVATION

The drive to succeed, especially in competition with others. Individuals who have a strong need for achievement seek out tasks that are moderately difficult.

98. EXTRINSIC MOTIVATION

Based upon external rewards or threats of punishment. For example, James tutors other students because he wants to earn money.

99. INTRINSIC MOTIVATION

Based upon personal enjoyment of a task or activity. For example, Robbie tutors other students because he enjoys helping them.

100. DISPLAY RULES

Cultural norms that influence how and when emotional responses are displayed.

101. JAMES-LANGE THEORY

Our subjective experience of emotion follows our experience of physiological changes ("We feel sorry because we cry").

102. **SCHACHTER-SINGER TWO-FACTOR THEORY**

     Physical arousal and cognitive labeling of that arousal produce our subjective experience of emotion.

103. **STRESS**

     An emotional response to demands that are perceived as threatening or exceeding a person's resources or ability to cope.

104. **CONFLICT**

     Occurs when a person is forced to choose between two or more opposing goals or desires. Conflict can be classified as approach-approach, avoidance-avoidance, or approach-avoidance.

105. **GENERAL ADAPTATION SYNDROME**

     Hans Selye's three-stage (alarm, resistance, exhaustion) reaction to chronic stress.

IX. DEVELOPMENTAL PSYCHOLOGY

106. **LONGITUDINAL METHOD**

     Measures a single individual or group of individuals over an extended period of time.

107. **CROSS-SECTIONAL METHOD**

     Compares individuals of various ages at one point in time.

108. **SCHEMA**

     A concept or framework that organizes and interprets information.

109. **ASSIMILATION**

     The process of absorbing new information into an existing schema.

110. **ACCOMMODATION**

     The process of adjusting old schemas or developing new ones to incorporate new information.

111. **OBJECT PERMANENCE**

     An infant's understanding that objects or people continue to exist even when they cannot be directly seen, heard, or touched.

112. IRREVERSIBILITY

    The child's inability to mentally reverse a sequence of events or logical operations.

113. CONSERVATION

    Understanding that certain physical characteristics (such as volume) remain unchanged, even when their outward appearance changes.

114. PERMISSIVE STYLE OF PARENTING

    Parents set few rules, make minimal demands, and allow their children to reach their own conclusions.

115. AUTHORITATIVE STYLE OF PARENTING

    Parents set firm rules, make reasonable demands, and listen to their child's viewpoint while still insisting on responsible behavior.

116. AUTHORITARIAN STYLE OF PARENTING

    Parents set rigid rules, enforce strict punishments, and rarely listen to their child's point of view.

117. PSYCHOSOCIAL STAGES

    Erik Erikson's theory that individuals pass through eight developmental stages, each involving a crisis that must be successfully resolved.

X. PERSONALITY

118. THE ID

    According to Freud, the id is completely unconscious. It consists of innate sexual and aggressive instincts and drives. The id is impulsive, irrational, and immature. It operates on a pleasure principle, seeking to achieve immediate gratification and avoid discomfort.

119. THE SUPEREGO

    According to Freud, the superego is partly conscious. It consists of internalized parental and societal standards. The superego operates on a morality principle, seeking to enforce ethical conduct.

120. THE EGO

According to Freud, the ego resides in the conscious and preconscious levels of awareness. The ego is rational and practical. It operates on a reality principle, seeking to mediate between the demands of the id and the superego.

121. DEFENSE MECHANISMS

In Freudian theory, the ego's protective method of reducing anxiety and distorting reality.

122. REPRESSION

Freud's first and most basic defense mechanism. Repression prevents unacceptable impulses from coming into conscious awareness.

123. SELF-EFFICACY

The feelings of self-confidence or self-doubt that people bring to a specific situation.

124. LOCUS OF CONTROL

Individuals who accept personal responsibility for their life experiences have an internal locus of control. Individuals who believe that most situations are governed by chance have an external locus of control.

125. FIVE-FACTOR MODEL

Trait theory of personality that includes openness, conscientiousness, extroversion, agreeableness, and neuroticism.

XI. TESTING AND INDIVIDUAL DIFFERENCES

126. G FACTOR

The notion, proposed by Charles Spearman, of a general intelligence factor that is responsible for a person's overall performance on tests of mental ability.

127. FLUID INTELLIGENCE

Aspects of innate intelligence, including reasoning abilities, memory, and speed of information processing, that are relatively independent of education and tend to decline as people age.

128. CRYSTALLIZED INTELLIGENCE

Knowledge and skills gained through experience and education that tend to increase over the life span.

129. STANDARDIZATION

Establishment of norms and uniform procedures for giving and scoring a test.

130. RELIABILITY

Measure of consistency and reproducibility of test scores during repeated administrations of a test.

131. VALIDITY

The ability of a test to measure what it is designed to measure.

132. SELF-FULFILLING PROPHECY

Observations or behaviors that result primarily from expectations.

XII. ABNORMAL BEHAVIOR

133. *DIAGNOSTIC AND STATISTICAL MANUAL OF MENTAL DISORDERS (DSM-5)*

Classification system developed by the American Psychiatric Association used to describe abnormal behaviors.

134. PHOBIAS

Characterized by a strong, irrational fear of specific objects or situations that are normally considered harmless.

135. OBSESSIVE-COMPULSIVE DISORDER

Characterized by persistent, repetitive, and unwanted thoughts (obsessions) and behaviors (compulsions).

136. POST-TRAUMATIC STRESS DISORDER

Characterized by intense feelings of anxiety, horror, and helplessness after experiencing a traumatic event such as a violent crime, natural disaster, or military combat.

137. BIPOLAR DISORDER

Characterized by periods of both depression and mania.

138. SOMATIC SYMPTOM AND RELATED DISORDERS

Characterized by physical complaints about conditions that are caused by psychological factors.

139. SCHIZOPHRENIA

Group of severe disorders involving major disturbances in perception, language, thought, emotion, and balance. Delusional beliefs, hallucinations, and disorganized speech and thought are three key characteristic symptoms.

140. NARCISSISTIC PERSONALITY DISORDER

Characterized by a grandiose sense of self-importance, fantasies of unlimited success, need for excessive admiration, and a willingness to exploit others to achieve personal goals.

141. DISSOCIATIVE DISORDERS

Involve a splitting apart of significant aspects of a person's awareness, memory, or identity. Dissociative amnesia is characterized by a partial or total inability to recall past experiences and important information. Some individuals with dissociative amnesia experience dissociative fugue, which is characterized by suddenly and inexplicably leaving home or wandering. Dissociative identity disorder (DID) is characterized by the presence of two or more distinct personality systems in the same individual.

XIII. TREATMENT OF ABNORMAL BEHAVIOR

142. PSYCHOANALYSIS

Freudian therapy designed to bring unconscious conflicts, which usually date back to childhood experiences, into consciousness.

143. COGNITIVE THERAPY

Therapy that treats problem behaviors and mental processes by focusing on faulty thought processes and beliefs.

144. RATIONAL EMOTIVE THERAPY

Albert Ellis's cognitive therapy to eliminate emotional problems through the rational examination of irrational beliefs.

145. HUMANISTIC THERAPY

Focuses on removing obstacles that block personal growth and potential.

146. CLIENT-CENTERED THERAPY

Carl Rogers's therapy emphasizing the client's natural tendency to become healthy and productive. Key techniques include empathy, unconditional positive regard, and active listening.

147. BEHAVIOR THERAPY

Group of techniques that use the principles of classical conditioning, operant learning, and observational learning to modify maladaptive behaviors.

148. SYSTEMATIC DESENSITIZATION

A gradual process of extinguishing a learned phobia by working through a hierarchy of fear-evoking stimuli while staying deeply relaxed.

149. AVERSION THERAPY

Uses the principles of classical conditioning to create anxiety by pairing an aversive stimulus with a maladaptive behavior.

150. BIOMEDICAL THERAPY

Uses drugs and electroconvulsive therapy to treat psychological disorders.

XIV. SOCIAL PSYCHOLOGY

151. FUNDAMENTAL ATTRIBUTION ERROR

The widespread tendency to overemphasize dispositional factors and to underestimate situational factors when making attributions about the cause of another person's behavior.

152. SELF-SERVING BIAS

The widespread tendency for people to take credit for their successes while at the same time attributing their failures to external situations beyond their control.

153. CENTRAL ROUTE TO PERSUASION

When people make decisions based upon factual information, logical arguments, and a thoughtful analysis of pertinent details. For example, you buy a cell phone based upon its price and number of available applications.

154. PERIPHERAL ROUTE TO PERSUASION

When people make decisions based upon emotional appeals and incidental cues. For example, you buy a cell phone based upon its color and catchy sales slogans.

155. FOOT-IN-THE-DOOR PHENOMENON

The persuasion strategy of getting a person to agree to a modest first request as a set-up for a later much larger request.

156. COGNITIVE DISSONANCE

The state of psychological tension, anxiety, and discomfort that occurs when an individual's attitude and behavior are inconsistent.

157. SOCIAL FACILITATION

The tendency for an individual's performance to improve when simple or well-rehearsed tasks are performed in the presence of others.

158. SOCIAL INHIBITION

The tendency for an individual's performance to decline when complex or poorly learned tasks are performed in the presence of others.

159. SOCIAL LOAFING

The phenomenon of people making less effort to achieve a goal when they work in a group rather than when they work alone.

160. DEINDIVIDUATION

The reduction of self-awareness and personal responsibility that can occur when a person is part of a group whose members feel anonymous.

161. BYSTANDER EFFECT

The tendency for individuals to be less likely to assist in an emergency situation when other people are present.

162. GROUP POLARIZATION

The tendency for a group's predominant opinion to become stronger or more extreme after an issue is discussed.

163. GROUPTHINK

The tendency for a cohesive decision-making group to ignore or dismiss reasonable alternatives.

164. CONFORMITY

The tendency for people to adopt the behavior, attitudes, and beliefs of other members of a group.

165. OBEDIENCE

The performance of an action in response to the direct orders of an authority or person of higher status.

PART II:
KEY CONTENT REVIEW

History and Approaches

 I. **WHAT IS PSYCHOLOGY?**

A. BASIC DEFINITION

1. *Psychology* is the **scientific** study of behavior and mental processes.
2. *Behavior* refers to any action or reaction of a living organism that can be directly observed.
3. *Mental processes* include internal processes such as thinking, feeling, and desiring that can be only indirectly observed.

B. GOALS

1. To describe particular behaviors by naming, classifying, and measuring them.
2. To explain why a behavior or mental process occurred.
3. To predict the conditions under which a future behavior or mental process is likely to occur.
4. To apply psychological knowledge to promote desired goals and prevent unwanted behaviors.

 II. **EARLY APPROACHES**

A. WILHELM WUNDT

1. Wilhelm Wundt (1832–1920) was a German scientist who established the first psychology research laboratory. Wundt wrote a landmark text and was the first person to call himself a "psychologist."

2. Wundt and his students conducted studies on the "elements" of consciousness, including sensation, perception, and emotion.
3. Wundt pioneered a research method called introspection in which his subjects reported detailed descriptions of their own conscious mental experiences.

B. STRUCTURALISM

1. Inspired by Wundt's ideas, Edward Titchener (1867–1927) established a psychological laboratory at Cornell University.
2. Titchener trained his students to use introspection to identify the most basic components, or structures, of conscious experiences.
3. Known as structuralism, Titchener's approach proved to be an unreliable method of investigation because different subjects often reported very different introspective findings about the same stimulus. In addition, introspection could not be used to study children, animals, or complex topics such as mental disorders.

C. FUNCTIONALISM

1. Led by Harvard professor William James (1842–1910), functionalists emphasized studying the purpose, or function, of behavior and mental experiences.
2. Functionalists rejected the introspective method of gathering information. For example, instead of asking subjects to describe the emotion of fear, functionalists studied how fear enables people and animals to adapt to their environments.
3. Functionalists broadened the scope of psychological research to include the direct observation of human and nonhuman animals.

D. PSYCHOANALYSIS

1. Both the structuralists and the functionalists focused on the study of conscious experiences. In contrast, the Austrian physician Sigmund Freud emphasized the role of unconscious conflicts in determining behavior and personality.

2. Known as psychoanalysis, Freud's school of psychological thought focused attention on conflicts between accepted norms of behavior and unconscious sexual and aggressive impulses.

3. Freud believed that dreams, "slips of the tongue" (called "Freudian slips"), and memory blocks all provide glimpses into the unconscious mind.

4. The modern psychodynamic approach incorporates many of Freud's landmark theories.

E. GESTALT

1. While the structuralists divided the object under study into a set of elements that could be analyzed separately, Gestalt psychologists focused on how we construct "perceptual wholes."

2. Gestalt theories and methodologies are used to explain perceptual organization. Chapter 6 will provide a detailed discussion of Gestalt theories.

III. MODERN PERSPECTIVES

A. THE BEHAVIORAL PERSPECTIVE

1. Behaviorists believe that both conscious and unconscious mental processes are unobservable. Instead, behaviorism focuses scientific investigations on observable behaviors that can be objectively measured. Behaviorists believe that human behavior is learned and can be controlled through the presence or absence of rewards and punishments.

2. Behaviorism emerged from the pioneering work of the Russian physiologist Ivan Pavlov (1849–1936). Pavlov conducted a series of famous experiments, which demonstrated that much behavior among animals is learned rather than instinctive. Pavlov's work will be studied in more depth in Chapter 8.

3. American psychologist John B. Watson (1878–1958) applied Pavlov's line of reasoning to human behavior. Watson believed that human beings could be socialized in any direction through learning. In 1924, he boldly declared,

"Give me a dozen healthy infants, well formed, and my own specified world to bring them up in, and I'll guarantee to take any one at random and train him to become any type of specialist I might select—doctor, lawyer, artist, merchant-chief, and, yes, even beggar and thief. . . ."

4. Watson's ideas had a great influence on the thinking of B. F. Skinner (1904–1990). Skinner's experiments and writings made him the leading advocate of behaviorism. Chapter 8 will provide a detailed discussion of Skinner's landmark work.

The behavioral perspective has generated significantly more multiple-choice questions than any of the other perspectives discussed in this chapter. Make sure that you know that Watson, Skinner, and other pioneering behaviorists stressed the importance of studying observable behavior. In addition, remember that behaviorist therapists use reinforcement to modify a client's behavior.

B. THE HUMANISTIC PERSPECTIVE

1. The American psychologist Carl Rogers (1902–1987) played a key role in the rise of humanistic psychology. Rogers believed that every person has the ability to self-actualize or reach their full potential. He emphasized the importance of free will and choice in human behavior. Chapter 12 will provide a detailed discussion of Rogers' work on personality.

2. Abraham Maslow (1908–1970) was another key leader in the development of humanistic psychology. Chapter 10 will examine Maslow's influential theory of motivation.

C. THE PSYCHODYNAMIC PERSPECTIVE

1. Freud's key theories about the unconscious continue to influence contemporary psychologists who follow the psychodynamic perspective. While continuing to emphasize the importance of unconscious influences, the psychodynamic perspective places less emphasis on sexual instincts.

2. The psychodynamic approach to therapy emphasizes repressed memories, free association, dream interpretation,

and analysis of transference. Psychodynamic ideas will be discussed in greater detail in Chapters 12 and 15.

D. THE BIOLOGICAL PERSPECTIVE

1. Psychologists who employ the biological perspective study the physical bases of human and animal behavior.
2. Chapter 5 will provide a detailed discussion of the nervous system and the endocrine system.

E. THE COGNITIVE PERSPECTIVE

1. The cognitive perspective focuses on the way humans gather, store, and process sensory information.
2. Influenced by the computer revolution, cognitive psychologists use an information-processing model to conceptualize human memory, thinking, and problem solving. Chapter 9 will provide an in-depth discussion of the cognitive perspective.

F. THE SOCIOCULTURAL PERSPECTIVE

1. The sociocultural perspective focuses on how culture and social situations affect the way people think, feel, and behave.
2. See Chapter 16 for an in-depth discussion of the key research studies and findings based on the sociocultural perspective.

G. THE EVOLUTIONARY PERSPECTIVE

1. The evolutionary perspective uses the principles of evolution to explain psychological processes and phenomena.
2. Evolutionary psychologists believe that natural selection plays a key role in determining human behavior. For example, evolutionary psychologists point to natural selection to explain the male preference for attractive, youthful spouses and the female preference for mates who possess high social status and financial resources. Chapter 5 will include a detailed discussion of the insights of the evolutionary perspective.

IV. A BROAD DISCIPLINE

A. DIVERSE SPECIALTY AREAS

1. Psychology embraces a wide range of specialty areas.
2. Clinical psychology and counseling attract the largest number of doctoral students.

B. SAMPLE CAREERS

1. Clinical psychology specializes in the evaluation, diagnosis, and treatment of mental and behavioral disorders.
2. Forensic psychology applies the principles of psychology to the legal profession, including jury selection and psychological profiling.
3. Educational psychology uses knowledge of how people learn to help develop instructional methods and materials.
4. Industrial-organizational psychology applies the principles of psychology to the workplace, including employee motivation, job satisfaction, and personnel selection.

Psychology includes a large number of subfields and career specialties. Note that AP Psychology test writers have written several multiple-choice questions devoted to industrial-organizational psychology. Psychologists who specialize in this area study such workplace conditions as employee evaluation, job satisfaction, and leadership styles.

Research Methods

I. THE EXPERIMENTAL METHOD

A. DEFINITION

1. An experiment is a carefully controlled method of investigation used to establish a cause-and-effect relationship.
2. The experimenter purposely manipulates and controls selected variables in order to determine cause and effect.

B. TESTABLE HYPOTHESIS

1. A hypothesis is a tentative statement that describes the relationship between two or more variables. A hypothesis must be testable, verifiable, and refutable.
2. The independent variable is the factor that is manipulated or controlled by the experimenter.
3. The dependent variable is the factor that is measured by the experimenter. It is affected by and thus dependent on the independent variable.
4. Examples
   ▸ *An experimenter wants to determine if playing violent video games increases the frequency of aggressive behavior in children. The independent variable in this study is the type of video game played. The dependent variable in this study is the amount of aggressive behavior exhibited by the children.*
   ▸ *An experimenter wants to determine the relationship between rehearsal/repetition of a list of definitions of difficult SAT vocabulary words and later recall of these definitions. The independent variable in this study is the*

amount of rehearsal/repetition. The dependent variable in this study is the recall of correct definitions.

▸ An experimenter wants to determine if a new drug reduces hyperactivity in children. The independent variable in this study is the drug. The dependent variable in this study is the level of hyperactivity.

5. Operational Definitions

▸ An operational definition is a precise description of how the variable in a study will be manipulated and measured.

▸ For example, in a study measuring the relationship between rehearsal/repetition and recall of difficult SAT vocabulary words, rehearsal might be operationally defined as the number of times the subject reads aloud a list of words. The difficult words might be operationally defined as answers to Level 5 SAT sentence completion questions. The recall might be operationally defined as the percentage of words that are correctly defined.

Independent and dependent variables are two of the most frequently tested concepts on the AP Psychology exam. Every released exam contains multiple-choice questions asking you to identify independent and dependent variables in a sample research design. In addition, as noted in Chapter 1, there is a better than 50–50 chance that your exam will include a free-response question asking you to design and/or describe an experiment. Your description must include a discussion of independent and dependent variables.

C. PARTICIPANTS: EXPERIMENTAL AND CONTROL GROUPS

1. The experimental group comprises the participants who are exposed to the independent variable.

2. The control group comprises the participants who are exposed to all experimental conditions except the independent variable. This enables the experimenter to make comparisons with the experimental group.

3. Confounding variables

▸ In a controlled experiment, confounding or extraneous variables are differences between the experimental

group and the control group other than the independent
variable. Confounding variables have an unwanted
influence on the outcome of an experiment.

▸ For example, in a study measuring the impact of playing
violent video games on the frequency of aggression in
children, confounding variables could include the income
level of the children's parents and the incidence of child
abuse.

D. EXPERIMENTAL CONTROLS

1. Purpose
   ▸ *Controls are used to ensure that all groups in the
   experiment are treated exactly the same, except for the
   independent variable.*

2. Problems
   ▸ *Experimenter bias occurs when a researcher's
   expectations or preferences about the outcome of a
   study influence the results in a hoped-for direction.*
   ▸ *Sample bias occurs when research participants are not
   representative of the larger population.*

3. Solutions
   ▸ *Random assignment—procedure by which participants
   are assigned to experimental and control groups by
   chance. This minimizes pre-existing differences between
   those assigned to the different groups.*
   ▸ *Placebo—an inactive substance or fake treatment often
   used as a control technique in drug research.*
   ▸ *Single-blind study—a procedure in which the subjects do
   not know whether they are in the experiment or control
   group.*
   ▸ *Double-blind study—a procedure in which neither
   the researcher nor the participant knows which group
   received the experimental treatment. This procedure
   reduces experimenter bias.*

E. ADVANTAGES OF EXPERIMENTS

1. Enable researchers to identify cause-and-effect relationships.
2. Enable researchers to distinguish between real and placebo
   effects.

3. Enable researchers to control bias by using a double-blind study.
4. Enable researchers to manipulate the independent variable and measure the dependent variable.
5. Enable researchers to replicate a study thus increasing confidence that the independent variable influences the dependent variable.

F. DISADVANTAGES OF EXPERIMENTS

1. Create artificial laboratory conditions that do not correspond to real-life situations.
2. Can be compromised by confounding variables that are difficult to identify and control.
3. Susceptible to researcher and participant biases.
4. Raise ethical concerns when subjects are deceived.

II. DESCRIPTIVE RESEARCH

A. DEFINITION

1. Descriptive research includes methods that enable researchers to observe and describe behaviors and mental processes without manipulating variables.
2. Descriptive methods do not enable researchers to establish cause-and-effect relationships.

B. SURVEYS

1. A research technique that uses questionnaires or interviews or a combination of the two to assess the behavior, attitudes, and opinions of a large number of people.
2. The entire group that a researcher wants to study is called a population.
3. Researchers generally question only a sample of the population whose opinions they seek to assess. A random sample, in which every person in the population has an equal chance of participating, helps minimize bias and ensure that the sample is representative.

4. It is important to note that survey respondents often report that they are healthier, happier, and less prejudiced than would be expected based upon the results of other types of research. This phenomenon is known as the social desirability bias.

C. NATURALISTIC OBSERVATION

1. In a naturalistic observation, researchers unobtrusively observe the behavior of subjects as it occurs in a real social setting.
2. Naturalistic observation provides a slice of life that can be very revealing. However, it is important to remember that naturalistic observations are descriptive and do not explain behavior.

D. CASE STUDIES

1. A case study is an in-depth examination of a single research participant.
2. Case studies enable researchers to obtain detailed knowledge about a person. They also provide an opportunity to conduct in-depth studies of rare and unusual cases.
3. Case studies cannot be used to establish cause-and-effect relationships. They are susceptible to inaccurate reporting and the subject's biased views.

E. STUDIES OF DEVELOPMENT

1. The longitudinal method measures a single individual or group of individuals over an extended period of time. For example, a longitudinal study of intelligence would retest the same people over a period of years. Longitudinal studies provide in-depth information but can be expensive and time-consuming.
2. The cross-sectional method compares individuals of various ages at one point in time. For example, a cross-sectional study of achievement motivation would test eighth, tenth, and twelfth grade students at the beginning of the school year. Cross-sectional studies provide information about age differences. However, it is very difficult to make

generalizations since cross-sectional studies measure behavior at only one point in time.

III. CORRELATION STUDIES

A. DEFINITION

1. In correlation studies researchers observe or measure a relationship between variables in which changes in one variable are reflected in changes in the other variable.
2. It is important to note that in correlation studies researchers do not directly manipulate the variables.
3. Correlations can be used to analyze the data gathered in any type of descriptive method.

B. CORRELATION COEFFICIENT

1. A correlation coefficient is a numerical value that indicates the strength and direction of the relationship between two variables.
2. Correlation coefficients are calculated by a formula that produces a number ranging from +1.00 to -1.00.
3. A positive correlation
    ‣ *Indicates that two variables move or vary in the same direction.*
    ‣ *For example, studies have found a positive relationship between smoking and the incidence of lung cancer. That is, as frequency of smoking increases so does the incidence of lung cancer.*
4. A negative correlation
    ‣ *Indicates that two variables move or vary in opposite directions.*
    ‣ *For example, studies have found a negative correlation between level of education and anger. That is, as level of education increases expressions of anger decrease.*
5. A zero correlation
    ‣ *Indicates that there is no relationship between two variables.*

▸ *For example, a study by Isabelle Deltour for the Danish Cancer Society found no correlation between cell phone use and incidence of brain tumors.*

Which of the following is the strongest correlation coefficient: −0.83, +0.10 or +0.64? The answer is −0.83. Remember that correlations become stronger as they approach either −1.0 or +1.0. A negative correlation of −0.83 means that there is a very strong inverse relationship. Remember, the strength of the correlation weakens as the correlation coefficient approaches 0.00.

C. CORRELATION AND CAUSATION

1. Correlation studies indicate the possibility of a cause-and-effect relationship.
2. Remember that correlation does not prove causation. For example, research studies have found a moderate correlation of +0.4 between SAT scores and college grades. However, this correlation does not tell us if high SAT scores cause high college grades. Other known and unknown factors, such as the level of achievement motivation and the presence or absence of tutors, could be responsible for both the SAT scores and the college grades.

D. ADVANTAGES OF CORRELATION STUDIES

1. They can be used to describe or clarify a relationship between two variables.
2. They can be an efficient way to utilize preexisting data.
3. They can be used to dispel illusory correlations. Although widely believed, an illusory correlation is in fact non-existent. For example, it is widely, but erroneously, believed that there is a correlation between date of birth and personality traits.

E. DISADVANTAGES OF CORRELATION STUDIES

1. They cannot be used to establish cause-and-effect relationships.

2. They cannot be used to establish the direction of causal influence.
3. They do not allow researchers to actively manipulate the variables.
4. They make it difficult to identify the impact of confounding variables.

IV. DESCRIPTIVE STATISTICS

A. MEASURES OF CENTRAL TENDENCY

1. Mean
   ‣ *The sum of a set of scores in a distribution divided by the number of scores. The mean is the average score.*
   ‣ *Extreme scores have a greater impact on the mean than on the mode or the median.*
   ‣ *Any change in the highest score in any distribution must result in a change in the mean.*
2. Median
   ‣ *The score that divides a frequency distribution exactly in half, so that the same number of scores lie on each side of it.*
3. Mode
   ‣ *The most frequently occurring score in a distribution.*

B. MEASURES OF VARIATION

1. Definition
   ‣ *A measure of variation is a single score that presents information about the spread of scores in a distribution.*
2. Range
   ‣ *The highest score in a distribution minus the lowest score.*
3. Standard deviation
   ‣ *The most widely used measure of variation.*
   ‣ *A standard measurement of how much the scores in a distribution deviate from the mean.*

4. Normal distribution
   ▸ *Normal distributions form a bell-shaped or symmetrical curve.*
   ▸ *In a normal distribution of test scores, the percentage of scores that fall at or above the mean score is 50. The percentage of test scores that fall at or below the mean score is also 50.*
   ▸ *In a normal distribution, approximately one-third of the scores fall one standard deviation below the mean and one-third of the scores fall one standard deviation above the mean. For example, the Wechsler IQ tests have a mean of 100 and a standard deviation of 15. This means that one-third of the people taking these tests will have scores between 85 and 100 and another third will have scores between 100 and 115.*
   ▸ *All score-based normal curves have the following 68–95–99.7 rule in common:*
      ▸ *Approximately 68% of all scores fall within one standard deviation of the mean.*
      ▸ *Approximately 95% of all scores fall within two standard deviations of the mean.*
      ▸ *Approximately 99.7% of all scores fall within three standard deviations of the mean.*
      ▸ *This distribution is shown in the following diagram:*

68–95–99.7 Rule for Normal Distribution

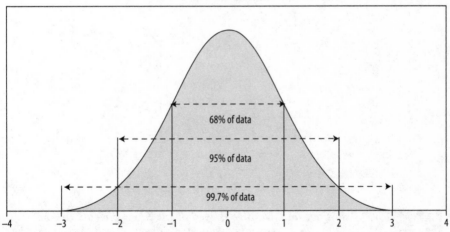

C. SKEWED DISTRIBUTIONS

1. Positively skewed distributions
   ▸ *A positively skewed distribution contains a preponderance of scores on the low end of the scale.*
   ▸ *The mean will be higher than the median in a positively skewed distribution. The median is thus a better representation of central tendency than the mean in a positively skewed distribution.*

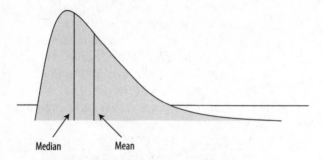

2. Negatively skewed distributions
   ▸ *A negatively skewed distribution contains a preponderance of scores on the high end of the scale.*
   ▸ *The mean will be lower than the median in a negatively skewed distribution. The median is thus a better representative of central tendency than the mean in a negatively skewed distribution.*

Positive and negative skewed distributions are easy to confuse. One way to remember what a positively skewed curve looks like is to visualize a "p" lying on its back. The preponderance of scores are to the left or the low end of the scale.

V. INFERENTIAL STATISTICS

A. KEY POINTS

1. Most experiments are conducted with a small sample of subjects.
2. Psychologists want to generalize the results from their small sample to a larger population.
3. Inferential statistics are used to determine how likely it is that a study's outcome is due to chance and whether the outcome can be legitimately generalized to the larger population from which the sample was selected.

B. THE P-VALUE

1. The p-value is the probability of concluding that a difference exists when in fact this difference does not exist.
2. A statistically significant difference is a difference not likely due to chance. By consensus, a statistically significant difference is one that would show up only 5 percent of the time or less.
3. The smaller the p-value, the more significant the results. A p-value can never equal 0 because researchers can never be 100 percent certain that the results did not occur due to chance.

VI. ETHICAL GUIDELINES

A. HUMAN RESEARCH STUDIES

1. Informed consent
   ▸ *Informed consent is the participant's agreement to take part in a study after being told what to expect.*
   ▸ *Researchers must obtain the participant's permission, or their parent's or guardian's permission before the study begins.*
2. Voluntary participation
   ▸ *All participation must be voluntary.*
   ▸ *Participants should be told that they are free to withdraw from the research at any time.*

3. Deception
   ▸ *The American Psychological Association (APA) recognizes the need for some deception in certain research areas.*
   ▸ *Deception is only justified when there is no alternative and the findings justify the use of deception because of scientific, educational, or applied value.*
   ▸ *When deception is used, subjects must be debriefed to explain the true purpose of the study and clear up any misconceptions or concerns.*

4. Confidentiality
   ▸ *All information about participants must remain private.*
   ▸ *Researchers may not compromise the privacy of their participants.*

5. Alternative activities
   ▸ *Many college courses include research participation as a course requirement or opportunity for extra credit.*
   ▸ *All students must be given an option to choose an alternative activity of equal value.*

B. ANIMAL RESEARCH STUDIES

1. Must have a clear scientific purpose.
2. Must provide humane living conditions for animal subjects.
3. Must legally acquire animal subjects from accredited companies.
4. Must employ the least amount of suffering feasible.
5. Note that less than 10 percent of research is done with nonhuman animals. Ninety percent of the nonhuman animals are rats, mice, and pigeons.

The Biological Bases of Behavior

I. Neural Communication

A. THE NEURON

1. The neuron is the fundamental building block of the nervous system. It uses both chemical and electrical signals to communicate messages to other neurons or muscles.

2. There are several components of the neuron:

   ▸ *Cell body or soma—the large portion of the neuron that contains the nucleus and the organelles; receives messages from the dendrites*

   ▸ *Dendrites—branch-like portions of a neuron that receive and communicate the nervous signal from the tips of neuron to the cell body.*

   ▸ *Axon—conduit that communicates the signal down the neuron and away from the cell body*

   ▸ *Myelin sheath—lipid/fat based insulation around the Schwann cells that stops the leaking of the electrical signal. The myelin sheath is formed by the Glial cells. The disease multiple sclerosis (MS) is caused by a deterioration of the myelin sheath which results in the loss of controlling muscle movement.*

   ▸ *Schwann cell—chain of cells that propagates the nervous signal*

   ▸ *Nodes of Ranvier—space or gap between the Schwann cells*

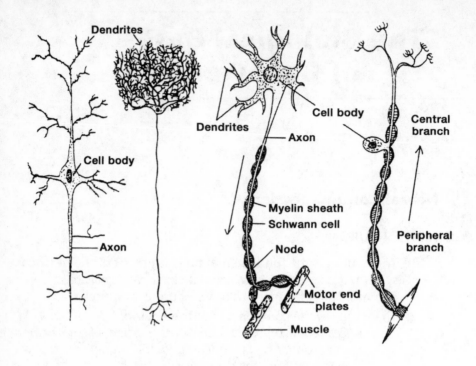

B. ACTION POTENTIAL

1. A brief electrical impulse by which information is transmitted along the axon of a neuron.
2. All neurons have a charge associated with them because of the concentration of various ions being transported into and out of the cell. A cell at rest has a resting membrane potential of approximately a -70mV. Both sodium and potassium channels are closed.
3. Depolarization—reduction in the absolute value of membrane potential because sodium channels open and flood inside the cell. Potassium channels are closed.
4. Action potential—if depolarization reaches the threshold, an action potential will be created and the neuron will fire. This is an example of the all-or-none response. It is important to note that the myelin sheath increases the velocity of conduction of the action potential along the axon.
5. Saltatory conduction—propagation of the chemical signal down the neuron from one node to the next.

6. Repolarization and hyperpolarization—decrease in membrane potential (more negative) because potassium channels open and potassium leaves the cell. Sodium channels are closed. Returns the membrane potential from positive (caused by depolarization) to negative.

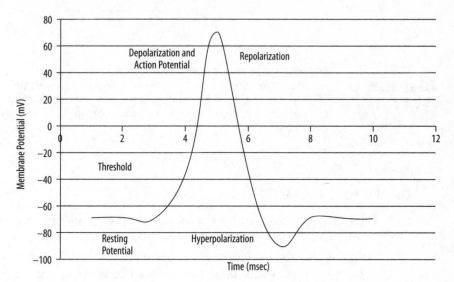

C. PASSAGE OF A NERVE TO A REFLEX ACTION

1. Synapse—the gap between nerve cells or a nerve cell and a muscle cell.

2. Synaptic vesicle—a small membrane-bound organelle that holds the neurotransmitter at the presynaptic membrane. The vesicle will eventually release the neurotransmitter into the synapse.

3. Presynaptic membrane—the surface of the synaptic terminal that faces the synaptic cleft or the space between neurons. The neurotransmitter (packaged in a vesicle) will be released across the cleft to the postsynaptic cell via the presynaptic membrane.

4. Postsynaptic Membrane—the surface of the cell body/axon that is on the opposite side of the synapse. It receives the

neurotransmitter and depolarization of the neuron will take place, thus propagating the signal.

Presynaptic Cell   Cleft   Postsynaptic Cell

Test Tip

Knowing the structure and function of the neuron is very important. Be sure you can identify and explain the function of dendrites, the myelin sheath, and the axon. It is interesting to note that the largest number of sensory neurons is found on our lips.

D. NEUROTRANSMITTERS

1. Neurotransmitters are chemical messengers manufactured by a neuron. They are released at the synaptic vesicles, which are tiny sacs located in the axon terminals.

2. The human body contains hundreds of substances known (or suspected) to function as neurotransmitters.

3. Endorphins are the best-known neurotransmitters. These chemicals can reduce pain or produce feelings of pleasure. For example, endorphins can help athletes overcome pain from an injury. They can also produce a boosted mood, which is often called "runner's high."

4. Neurotransmitters play a role in your eating habits and body weight. When levels of norepinephrine, dopamine, serotonin, leptin and other neurotransmitters are low, hunger and or eating results. When levels of these substances are high, satiety, or fullness, results.

5. Neurotransmitters may play a role in influencing or causing psychological disorders. The following chart lists the key neurotransmitters that have generated multiple-choice questions on the AP Psychology exam:

Neurotransmitter	Functions	Disease Associated With
Dopamine	Movement Thought processes	Parkinson's disease Schizophrenia
Serotonin	Emotional state Sleep	Depression Anxiety OCD (obsessive compulsive disorder)
Norepinephrine	Physical arousal Learning and memory	High blood pressure Anxiety
Acetylcholine	Learning and memory Muscle contraction	Alzheimer's Disease Muscular disorders
GABA (gamma-aminobutyric acid)	Inhibition of brain activity	Anxiety
Endorphins (natural pain killers)	Pain Perception	Opiate addiction (pain-killing drugs)

KEY CONTENT REVIEW

Test Tip

The AP Psychology exam includes a number of multiple-choice questions that focus on the link between selected neurotransmitters and psychological disorders. Be sure you know that acetylcholine is linked to Alzheimer's disease, that excess dopamine is linked with schizophrenia, and that too little dopamine is linked to Parkinson's disease.

E. DRUG EFFECTS ON NERVOUS SYSTEM

1. Psychoactive drugs have inhibitory or excitatory effects on the nervous system.
2. Agonists are drugs that mimic the effect of the neurotransmitter.

3. Antagonists are drugs that inhibit the effect of the neurotransmitter.

4. Prozac is an antidepressant drug that works as an agonist of serotonin.

5. Many psychoactive drugs have side effects because the drug of choice may work on different neural pathways. For example, Prozac treats depression, but can alter sleep, eating patterns, and other thought processes.

 ## II. Nervous System

A. THE CENTRAL NERVOUS SYSTEM (CNS)

1. Comprised of the brain and the spinal cord, the central nervous system is considered to be the command center of the body.

2. The spinal cord deals with reflex or involuntary actions. Spinal cord injuries can produce paralysis of limbs. The higher the site of the damage on the spinal cord, the more severe the injury.

3. A common reflex is known as the "knee-jerk" reflex. This reflex is tested by tapping just below the knee, causing the lower leg to suddenly jerk forward. Often used by doctors in performing a clinical neurologic exam.

4. The brain is required for voluntary movements.

B. THE PERIPHERAL NERVOUS SYSTEM (PNS)

1. The peripheral nervous system connects the CNS with the rest of the body through nerves.

2. The peripheral nervous system carries incoming messages to your brain and outgoing signals to your body's muscles and glands.

3. For example, as you cross a traffic-filled street, your PNS will notice the auditory sounds of cars and the visual patterns of oncoming traffic. Your brain assesses the situation and tells your body that danger may be lingering, so you cross the street with caution.

C. THE SOMATIC DIVISION OF THE PNS

1. The somatic division of the PNS allows communication with the outside world. It carries information to the CNS and sends voluntary signals to your muscles. For example, if you smell a food that gives you an arousal, your muscles are then induced to eat the food.

D. THE AUTONOMIC DIVISION OF THE PNS

1. The autonomic division of the PNS carries information to the CNS and sends voluntary signals to your muscles.

2. The autonomic division regulates digestion, respiration, sleep, and other vital functions.

   ▸ *Sympathetic nervous system—the part of the autonomic nervous system (ANS) responsible for arousing the body and mobilizing its energy during times of stress. Activation of the sympathetic nervous system results in an increase in respiratory and heart rates and dilation of pupils. The "fight-or-flight" response of the sympathetic nervous system allows you to either attack or flee from a situation.*

   ▸ *Parasympathetic nervous system—the part of the autonomic nervous system that allows a person to return to a calm and collected state after arousal from the sympathetic division.*

 ## III. Endocrine System

A. THE ENDOCRINE SYSTEM IS A SYSTEM OF HORMONES THAT CARRIES MESSAGES THROUGH DIFFERENT GLANDS.

B. MAJOR GLANDS AND TISSUES

1. Hypothalamus—links the nervous and endocrine systems by receiving signals and propagating the endocrine response. Located in the lower half of the brain, it also allows humans to sense a need such as thirst or hunger.

2. Pituitary gland—known as the "master gland" because it regulates the activity of several other glands. The pituitary gland is under the control of the hypothalamus.

3. Thyroid gland—located near the trachea.

4. Parathyroid gland—located on the surface of the thyroid gland.

5. Pancreas—located near the kidneys; contains specialized cells called Islets of Langerhans that secrete hormones.

6. Adrenal glands—located on top of the kidneys. In an emergency, the adrenal glands secrete hormones that cause an increase in heart rate, blood pressure, and sugar levels, while simultaneously reducing blood flow to the digestive system.

7. Gonads—testes and ovaries.

8. Pineal gland—small peanut-shaped gland near the center of the brain.

9. Thymus—located in the upper portion of the chest cavity.

Test Tip

The nervous system and the endocrine system typically generate one or two multiple-choice questions on each exam. Be sure you understand the difference between the sympathetic and parasympathetic nervous systems. In addition, be sure you understand the functions of the pituitary gland and the adrenal glands.

C. TABLE OF MAJOR GLANDS, HORMONES SECRETED AND THE ACTIONS THAT ARE CONTROLLED

Gland	Hormone	Action
Pituitary	Oxytocin	Contraction of uterus; breast milk let-down
Pituitary	Antidiuretic hormone	Water retention in kidneys
Pituitary	Growth hormone	Stimulates growth
Pituitary	Prolactin	Stimulates milk production from mammary gland

Gland	Hormone	Action
Pituitary	Follicle stimulating hormone	Stimulates production of ova and sperm
Pituitary	Luteinizing hormone	Stimulates ovaries
Pituitary	Thyroid Stimulating hormone	Stimulates the thyroid
Thyroid	Triiodothyronine (T_3) and thyroxine (T_4)	Stimulates metabolism
Thyroid	Calcitonin	Lowers calcium level in bloodstream; stimulates bone construction
Parathyroid	Parathyroid hormone	Raises blood calcium
Pancreas	Insulin	Lowers blood glucose
Pancreas	Glucagon	Raises blood glucose
Adrenal Gland	Norepinephrine and Epinephrine	Causes fight-or-flight response to emergency situations; stimulates metabolism
Testes	Androgens	Promotes sperm formation and secondary male characteristics
Ovaries	Estrogens	Stimulate uterine lining and secondary female characteristics
Ovaries	Progesterone	Stimulate uterine lining growth; maintains pregnancy
Pineal	Melatonin	Maintains sleep-wake cycle and other circadian rhythms

KEY CONTENT REVIEW

IV. The Brain

A. TOOLS FOR BRAIN RESEARCH

1. The electroencephalogram (EEG)
   ▸ *Electrical activity throughout the brain sweeps in regular waves across its surface.*
   ▸ *The EEG records the patterns of these waves.*
   ▸ *The EEG reveals areas of the brain that are most active during a particular task or changes in mental states.*
   ▸ *The EEG can trace abnormal brain waves caused by brain malfunctions such as epilepsy.*

2. Positron Emission Tomography (PET) scan
   ▸ *Researchers inject a harmless, radioactive form of glucose into a person's bloodstream.*
   ▸ *The PET scan produces computer-generated, color-coded images of the brain that provide information about glucose metabolism.*
   ▸ *Originally designed to detect abnormalities, PET scans are now also used to identify brain areas active during ordinary activities.*

3. Computerized Tomography (CT) scan
   ▸ *Uses X-rays to create a static picture of the brain.*
   ▸ *Widely used in research because it is the least expensive type of imaging.*
   ▸ *CT scans reveal the effects of strokes, tumors, and other brain disorders.*

4. Magnetic Resonance Imaging (MRI)
   ▸ *Uses a high-frequency magnetic field to produce detailed, high-resolution pictures of the brain.*
   ▸ *MRI images are used to map brain structures and identify abnormalities.*

B. THE HINDBRAIN

1. The hindbrain is a region at the base of the brain that includes the medulla, the pons, and the cerebellum. The hindbrain is the oldest part of the brain to develop in evolutionary terms and controls such automatic behaviors as respiration and heartbeat.

2. Medulla
   ▸ Controls vital life functions such as breathing, circulation, and swallowing.

3. Pons
   ▸ Pons is Latin for "bridge."
   ▸ Located above the medulla, the pons contains axons that cross from one side of the brain to the other.
   ▸ The pons is responsible for sleeping, walking, and dreaming.

4. Cerebellum
   ▸ A large, two-sided hindbrain structure that is located at the back of the brain.
   ▸ Responsible for coordinating fine muscle movement and maintaining posture and equilibrium.

C. THE MIDBRAIN

1. The midbrain is a small area in the brain located just above the spinal cord and below the forebrain. The midbrain integrates auditory and visual sensory information and muscle movements.

2. The reticular formation is a network of nerve fibers that run through the center of the midbrain. The reticular formation helps regulate attention, arousal, and sleep. Without the reticular formation, you would not be alert or even conscious.

D. THE FOREBRAIN

1. The forebrain is the largest and most complex brain region. It contains centers for complex behaviors and mental processes.

2. Thalamus
   - *The thalamus is located at the top of the brainstem.*
   - *The thalamus receives input from all of the senses, except smell, and directs this information to the appropriate cortical areas.*
   - *Injury to the thalamus can cause blindness and deafness.*

3. Hypothalamus
   - *The hypothalamus is located under the thalamus. (The Latin word* hypo *means "under" or "beneath".)*
   - *Although only about the size of a peanut, the hypothalamus is often called the brain's "master control center" because it regulates key body functions such as hunger and thirst. Since the hypothalamus regulates both eating and satiety, damage to the hypothalamus can increase eating or produce a feeling of fullness.*

4. Hippocampus
   - *The hippocampus plays a key role in forming new memories of events and information.*

5. Amygdala
   - *The amygdala is linked to the production and regulation of emotions such as aggression, fear, and disgust.*

6. The Limbic System
   - *The hippocampus, the amygdala, and the hypothalamus are all part of the limbic system and play a key role in the experience of emotions.*

E. THE CEREBRAL CORTEX

1. The word "cortex" means "bark." Like the bark of a tree, the cerebral cortex is the thin (about one quarter of an inch) outer covering of the forebrain.

2. Gray and wrinkled, the cerebral cortex is composed of approximately 30 billion densely-packed neurons and nine times as many supporting glial cells. The grayish color explains why the cerebral cortex is often described as being composed of gray matter!

3. The wrinkles (also known as convolutions) significantly increase the brain's available surface area. If the cerebral cortex were not wrinkled, it would cover an area the size of a standard newspaper page.

4. The cerebral cortex is divided into left and right hemispheres. Each hemisphere controls the opposite side of the body. Thus, the left hemisphere controls the right side of the body, while the right hemisphere controls the left side of the body.

5. The two hemispheres have specialized functions. The left hemisphere specializes in verbal and analytical functions. The right hemisphere focuses on nonverbal abilities, such as visual recognition tasks and music. The following chart summarizes the functions of the left and right hemispheres:

Left Hemisphere	Right Hemisphere
Positive emotions	Negative emotions
Controls muscles for speech	Response to commands
Controls movements	Memory for shapes
Spontaneity	Memory for music
Memory for words and numbers	Understanding spatial relationships
Understanding speech and writing	Understanding images

6. Corpus callosum
   ▸ *The corpus callosum is a bundle of nerve fibers that connect the brain's left and right hemispheres.*
   ▸ *In rare cases, neurosurgeons prevent the spread of severe epileptic seizures by cutting the corpus callosum. Known as split-brain surgery, this procedure disrupts the communication between the left and right hemispheres.*

▸ *Split-brain patients provide a valuable source of information on how the two hemispheres function.*

F. AREAS OF THE CEREBRAL CORTEX

1. The two cerebral hemispheres are divided into eight distinct areas, or lobes—four in each hemisphere. Although their functions overlap, each lobe performs specialized tasks.

2. Frontal lobes
   ▸ *The two frontal lobes are located directly behind your forehead. The frontal lobes are responsible for abstract thought and emotional control. For example, the frontal lobes are invaluable in the mental process of weighing the consequences of an important decision. People who suffer damage to the frontal lobes may lose the ability to make and carry out plans.*
   ▸ *The left frontal lobe contains an area, known as Broca's area, that plays a crucial role in speech production. An individual with damage to Broca's area would have difficulty making the muscle movements needed for speech.*

3. Parietal lobes
   ▸ *The two parietal lobes are located at the top of the brain, just behind the frontal lobes.*
   ▸ *The parietal lobes receive and interpret bodily sensations, such as pressure, temperature, touch, pain, and the location of body parts.*

4. Temporal lobes
   ▸ *The two temporal lobes are located on each side of the brain above the ears. (The word "temporal" is Latin for "pertaining to the temples.")*
   ▸ *The temporal lobes process incoming sensory information from the ears.*
   ▸ *The left temporal lobe contains an area, known as Wernicke's area, that plays a crucial role in language development. An individual with damage to Wernicke's area would have difficulty comprehending a spoken request for directions.*

5. Occipital lobes
    ‣ *The two occipital lobes are located at the back of the brain.*
    ‣ *The occipital lobes are responsible for vision and visual perception.*
    ‣ *Damage to the occipital lobes can produce blindness, even if the eyes are undamaged.*

AP Psychology test writers know that you are not studying to be a brain surgeon. Relax, you will not be asked to label a diagram of the brain or write a free-response essay listing all of the lobes or parts of the forebrain. However, you are expected to know the functions of the hypothalamus, the hippocampus, the amygdala, the corpus callosum, and the occipital and temporal lobes. Taken together, these six parts of the brain have generated almost half of the multiple-choice questions asked about the brain.

KEY CONTENT REVIEW

Sensation and Perception

I. INTRODUCTION

A. SENSATION

1. The process by which our sensory receptors respond to light, sound, odor, textures, and taste and transmit that information to the brain.

2. Our eyes, ears, nose, tongue, and skin comprise an elaborate sensory system that receives and processes information from the environment.

3. Each sense organ contains specialized cells called receptors which detect and then convert light waves, sound waves, chemical molecules, and pressure into neural impulses that are transmitted to the brain.

4. When adults are totally deprived of sensory input for long periods of time, they experience hallucinations and impaired efficiency in all areas of intellectual functioning.

B. PERCEPTION

1. The process by which the brain actively selects, organizes, and assigns meaning to incoming neural messages sent from sensory receptors.

2. For example, from a sensory point of view, the American flag is a mass of red, white, and blue colors and horizontal and vertical lines. Perception is the process by which you interpret these splotches of color and array of lines as the American flag.

II. BASIC PRINCIPLES OF SENSATION

A. TRANSDUCTION

1. The process by which sensory receptors convert the incoming physical energy of stimuli such as light waves into neural impulses that the brain can understand.

2. As noted by psychologist Philip Zimbardo, the transduction "process seems so immediate and direct that it fools us into assuming that the sensation of redness is characteristic of a tomato or the sensation of cold is characteristic of ice cream." In reality, sensations such as "red" and "cold" occur only when the neural impulses reach the brain.

B. THRESHOLDS

1. Absolute threshold
   ▸ *The minimum amount of a stimulus that an observer can reliably detect at least 50 percent of the time.*
   ▸ *For example, the human visual system can barely detect a candle flame at a distance of about 30 miles on a clear, dark night.*

2. Difference Threshold
   ▸ *The minimal difference needed to notice a stimulus change.*
   ▸ *The difference threshold is also called the "just noticeable difference" or JND.*
   ▸ *For example, Ben is trying to study for an AP Psychology test on sensation and perception. However, he can't concentrate because his sister is watching Gossip Girl and has the volume turned at full blast. Ben asks Charlotte to "please turn the volume down so I can study!" Charlotte responds by lowering the volume by one notch. If Ben notices this minimal amount of change, it qualifies as a just noticeable difference. Needless to say, Ben will probably not be satisfied with a just noticeable difference and will soon demand that Charlotte turn the TV volume down some more.*

3. Weber's law
   ▸ *The German psychologist Ernst Weber (1795–1878) observed that the just noticeable difference will vary depending on its relation to the original stimulus.*

▸ *According to Weber's law, the size of the just noticeable difference is proportional to the strength of the original stimulus. For example, for the average person to perceive their difference, two objects must differ in weight by 2 percent.*

▸ *For example, a weight lifter who is bench pressing 50 pounds would notice the addition of a 5-pound weight. However, the same weight lifter would not notice the extra 5 pounds if he were bench pressing 500 pounds.*

C. SIGNAL DETECTION THEORY

1. A problem with traditional thresholds

▸ *The traditional theory of thresholds assumed that if a signal were intense enough to exceed one's absolute threshold, it would be sensed. If the same signal were below our threshold, it would be missed.*

▸ *The traditional theory of thresholds did not take into account the characteristics of the perceiver. For example, Ben noticed the change in volume when Charlotte turned her TV down one notch because he was trying to concentrate and was focused on the TV's distracting noise. Had Ben been playing a video game with a friend, he would not have noticed the change in volume.*

2. A new theory

▸ *Signal detection theory assumes that there is no single absolute threshold. Instead, a detection depends upon a combination of stimulus intensity, background noise, and a person's physical condition, biases, and level of motivation. For example, a sentry in wartime will likely detect fainter stimuli than the same sentry in peacetime.*

▸ *When they are applying signal detection theory to experiments, psychologists sort the trials into one of four categories. If the signal is present, the person can decide that it is present or absent. These outcomes are called hits or misses. If the signal is absent, the person can still decide that the signal is either present or absent. These are called false alarms or correct rejections.*

D. SENSORY ADAPTATION

1. Sensory adaptation occurs when a constant stimulus is presented for a length of time. When this happens receptors fire less frequently and the sensation often fades or disappears.

2. Examples
   ▸ *When a jogger first puts on a new pair of running shoes, he or she immediately notices that the new shoes have a different feel from the old shoes. However, after going for a jog, he or she no longer notices the new shoes.*
   ▸ *When a swimmer first dives into a pool, he or she immediately notices that the water is chilly. However, after swimming a few laps, he or she no longer notices the water temperature.*

3. It is interesting to note that sensory adaptation does not affect our vision. The reason is because our eyes constantly shift from one location to another. This ensures that receptor cells in the eyes always receive continuously changing stimuli.

Test Tip

The basic processes of sensation generate a significant number of multiple-choice questions. Make sure that you can define and illustrate transduction, absolute threshold, signal detection theory, and sensory adaptation.

III. THE HUMAN VISUAL SYSTEM

A. INTRODUCTION

1. The visual system is our most complex and most important sense.

2. The visual system transduces light waves into neural messages that the brain then processes into what we consciously see.

B. FROM THE CORNEA TO THE RETINA

1. Cornea
   ▸ *Light waves from the outside world first enter the eye through the cornea.*

▸ *The cornea is a clear membrane covering the visible part of the eye. It protects the eye and helps gather and direct incoming light waves.*

2. Pupil

▸ *The small opening in the middle of the iris*
▸ *The pupil changes size to let in different amounts of light.*

3. Iris

▸ *The colored part of the eye*
▸ *The iris is actually a ring of muscle tissue that contracts or expands to control the size of the pupil. The muscles in the eye respond to light and to inner emotions. The pupils constrict when we are in parasympathetic calm and dilate when we are in sympathetic arousal.*

4. Lens

▸ *A transparent structure located behind the pupil that actually focuses and bends light as it enters the eye.*
▸ *Accommodation is the change in the curvature of the lens that enables the eye to focus on objects at various distances. Nearsightedness is a visual acuity problem that results when the cornea and lens focus on an image in front of the retina. As a result, distant objects appear blurry. Farsightedness is a visual acuity problem that results when the cornea and lens focus an image behind the retina. As a result, objects near the eye appear blurry.*

C. THE ALL-IMPORTANT RETINA

1. The retina is the light-sensitive membrane at the back of the eye. The retina contains millions of sensory receptors for vision. The transduction of light waves into neural messages occurs in the retina.

2. Rods

▸ *Photoreceptors in the retina that are especially sensitive to dim light but not to colors.*
▸ *Rods allow you to see in poorly lit environments. Cats have better night vision than humans because they have a higher proportion of rods to cones than do humans.*

3. Cones

▸ *Photoreceptors in the retina that are especially sensitive to colors and to bright light.*

▸ *Cones are concentrated in the center of the retina, in a small region called the fovea. Images that do not fall on the fovea tend to be perceived as blurry or indistinct.*

4. Bipolar cells
   ▸ *Specialized neurons that connect the rods and cones with the ganglion cells.*

5. Ganglion cells
   ▸ *Specialized neurons that connect to the bipolar cells. The bundled axons of the ganglion cells form the optic nerve.*

6. Blind spot
   ▸ *The point where the optic nerve leaves the eye and where there are no rods or cones.*
   ▸ *Because there are no rods or cones, we have a tiny hole, or blind spot in our vision. Normally, we are unaware of the blind spot because our eyes are always moving.*

D. THE VISUAL CORTEX

1. The optic nerve carries visual information to the brain's visual cortex.
2. The visual cortex lies in the occipital lobe at the back of the brain.

E. COLOR VISION

1. Introduction
   ▸ *The human visual system can identify approximately 7 million different color combinations. How does normal color vision work?*
   ▸ *Two theories describe how color vision works at different stages of the visual process.*

2. The trichromatic or three-color theory
   ▸ *The trichromatic theory begins with the fact that there are three primary colors—red, green, and blue. Any color can be created by combining the light waves of these three colors.*
   ▸ *In the mid-nineteenth century, the German physicist Hermann von Helmholtz (1821–1894) proposed that the eye must have color receptors that correspond to the three primary colors.*

▸ *Years later, researchers confirmed that the retina does have cones especially sensitive to the three primary colors.*

3. The opponent-process theory

▸ *The trichromatic theory explains how color processing works in the cones. However, it does not explain what happens in the ganglion cells and the rest of the visual system.*

▸ *According to the opponent-process theory, the ganglion cells process color in opposing pairs of red or green, black or white, and blue or yellow colors. The visual cortex also encodes color in terms of these three opponent pairs.*

▸ *The opponent-process theory explains a phenomena known as afterimages. An afterimage is the visual experience that occurs after the original source of stimulation is no longer present. For example, if you stare at a green, black, and yellow flag, you will soon tire your neural response to these colors. If you then look at a white sheet of paper, you will see an afterimage composed of the opposing red, white, and blue colors.*

F. COLOR BLINDNESS

1. Color blindness is a genetic disorder that prevents an individual from distinguishing between certain colors. People who are color blind typically have a deficiency in their cones.

2. The most common form of color blindness is related to deficiencies in the red-green system.

3. It is very rare to see no color at all. There have only been about 500 reported cases of total color blindness.

IV. THE HUMAN AUDITORY SYSTEM

A. INTRODUCTION

1. Hearing plays a vital role in language development and social interactions. It also alerts us to dangerous situations.

2. The auditory system transduces sound waves into neural messages that the brain then processes into what we consciously hear.

KEY CONTENT REVIEW

B. THE OUTER EAR

1. The outer ear collects sound waves.
2. The pinna
    ▸ *The flap of skin and cartilage attached to each side of our head.*
    ▸ *The pinna catches sound waves and channels them into the auditory canal.*
3. The auditory canal
    ▸ *Sound waves travel down the auditory canal and bounce into the ear drum.*
4. The eardrum or tympanic membrane
    ▸ *A tightly stretched membrane located at the end of the auditory canal.*
    ▸ *The eardrum vibrates when hit by sound waves. The vibrations of the eardrum match the intensity and frequency of the incoming sound waves.*

C. THE MIDDLE EAR

1. The middle ear amplifies sound waves.
2. Hammer, anvil, and stirrup
    ▸ *Three tiny bones in the middle ear*
    ▸ *Their joint action doubles the amplification of sound*
3. Oval window
    ▸ *The stirrup transmits the amplified vibrations to the oval window.*
    ▸ *The oval window is a small membrane separating the middle ear from the inner ear. It relays the vibrations to the cochlea.*

D. THE INNER EAR

1. The inner ear transduces sound waves into neural messages.
2. Cochlea
    ▸ *A spiral-shaped, fluid-filled structure that contains the basilar membrane and hair cells.*
    ▸ *It is interesting to note that the word* cochlea *comes from the Greek word for "snail."*
3. Basilar membrane
    ▸ *Runs the length of the cochlea*
    ▸ *Holds the hair cell receptors for hearing*

4. Hair cells
> ▸ *Sensory receptors embedded in the basilar membrane*
> ▸ *The hair cells transduce the physical vibration of the sound waves into neural impulses.*

E. THE BRAIN

1. As the hair cells bend, they stimulate the cells of the auditory nerve.
2. The auditory nerve carries the neural messages to the thalamus and then to the temporal lobe's auditory cortex.

F. DISTINGUISHING PITCH

1. Pitch is the relative highness or lowness of a sound.
2. Frequency theory
> ▸ *According to the frequency theory, the basilar membrane vibrates at the same frequency as the sound wave.*
> ▸ *The frequency theory explains how low-frequency sounds are transmitted to the brain.*
> ▸ *However, since individual neurons cannot fire faster than about 1000 times per second, the frequency theory does not explain how the much faster high-frequency sounds are transmitted.*
3. Place theory
> ▸ *According to place theory, different frequencies excite different hair cells at different locations along the basilar membrane.*
> ▸ *High-frequency sounds cause maximum vibrations near the stirrup end of the basilar membrane. Lower-frequency sounds cause maximum vibrations at the opposite end.*

G. THE LOSS OF HEARING

1. Conduction deafness
> ▸ *Caused when the tiny bones in the middle ear are damaged and cannot transmit sound waves to the inner ear.*
> ▸ *Hearing aids can amplify sound and help overcome conduction deafness.*

2. Nerve deafness
   ▸ *Caused by damage to the cochlea, hair cells, or auditory nerve.*
   ▸ *Exposure to noises such as headphones playing at full blast can damage hair cells and cause permanent hearing loss.*
   ▸ *Hearing aids cannot help nerve deafness since damage to the hair cells and auditory nerve is almost always irreversible.*

V. THE CHEMICAL SENSES

A. INTRODUCTION

1. Smell and taste are sometimes referred to as the chemical senses because they respond to chemical molecules rather than to forms of energy such as light and sound waves.
2. Smell and taste receptors are located near each other and often interact. As a result, we often have difficulty separating the two sensations.

B. SMELL OR OLFACTION

1. The mucous membrane at the top of each nostril contains receptor cells that absorb airborne chemical molecules. Our olfactory receptors can detect over 10,000 distinct smells. This ability can help us detect odors ranging from fragrant flowers to dangerous leaking gas.
2. The receptor cells communicate neural messages to the olfactory bulb.
3. It is important to note that unlike all other bodily sensations, impulses from the olfactory bulb do not go to the thalamus. Instead, the nerve fibers from the olfactory bulb connect to the brain at the amygdala and then to the hippocampus. This direct connection to these limbic system structures may explain why smell is capable of triggering such vivid memories and emotions.

C. TASTE OR GUSTATION

1. Our tongue is covered with bumps called papillae. The papillae are in turn covered with taste buds. Taste buds are also found in the palate at the back of the throat.

2. Humans have four major taste sensations—sweet, sour, salty, and bitter. In recent years, researchers have added *umami* (meaning "delicious" or "savory") to this traditional list. *Umami* is associated with the taste of protein found in meats and meat broths.

3. Although taste is often called the least critical of our senses, it can play an important survival role by helping us avoid eating or drinking harmful substances. On a positive note, taste (aided by smell) plays an important role in our enjoyment of everything from savory fruits to delicious desserts!

 VI. SKIN AND BODY SENSES

A. INTRODUCTION

1. Skin senses
   ‣ *Skin is our largest and heaviest sense organ.*
   ‣ *Skin protects our internal organs, holds body fluids, produces sensations of touch, warmth, and cold and provides essential information about pain.*

2. Body senses
   ‣ *Body senses provide essential information about your position and orientation in space.*

B. SKIN SENSES

1. Touch
   ‣ *Touch or pressure receptors are not evenly distributed among the different areas of our bodies. For example, they are more densely concentrated in the hands, face, and lips than on the legs or back.*
   ‣ *Touch plays a particularly important role in human relationships by helping communicate feelings of support, conformity, and love.*

2. Pain
   - ▸ *Pain is the unpleasant sensation of physical discomfort or suffering.*
   - ▸ *Pain plays a key survival role by warning about potential or actual injuries.*

3. The gate-control theory of pain
   - ▸ *According to the gate-control theory, the brain regulates pain by sending signals down the spinal cord that either open or close sensory pathways or "gates."*
   - ▸ *If the brain signals the gates to open, pain is experienced or intensified.*
   - ▸ *If the brain signals the gates to close, pain is reduced.*
   - ▸ *Psychological factors such as anxiety and fear can intensify pain while positive emotions such as laughter can help minimize pain.*

C. THE VESTIBULAR SENSE

1. The vestibular sense provides a sense of balance and equilibrium.
2. The inner ear contains receptors that are especially important for maintaining balance.
3. The semicircular canals are filled with fluid and lined with hairlike receptor cells that shift in response to motion. They provide the brain with important information about the body's posture and head position.
4. The vestibular and auditory systems are alike in that both depend upon hair cells to transduce a stimulus into neural messages.

Test Tip

Because of the importance of the retina and cochlea, it is easy to overlook the semicircular canals. Don't make this mistake. Be sure you know that the semicircular canals are located in the inner ear and are closely associated with the vestibular sense of balance.

VII. **SELECTION**

A. INTRODUCTION

1. Selecting where to direct our attention is the first step in perception.
2. Selective attention and feature detectors help explain why we pay attention to some stimuli in our environment and not to others.

B. SELECTIVE ATTENTION

1. Selective attention is the cognitive process of selectively concentrating on one or more aspects of the environment while filtering out or ignoring other information.
2. Examples
   ▸ *Gavin is playing a new video game with his friend. He doesn't hear his mother call for him to come to dinner. However, he does respond when his cell phone rings because he is expecting a call from his girlfriend.*
   ▸ *Chloe is the star guard on her high school basketball team. During a big game she doesn't hear the fans cheering for her. However, she does respond when her coach calls out a special play for her to run.*

C. FEATURE DETECTORS

1. The brain contains specialized neurons called feature detectors that respond only to certain sensory information.
2. David Hubel and Torsten Wiesel demonstrated that specialized neurons in the occipital lobe's visual cortex have the ability to respond to specific features of an image such as angles, lines, curves, and movements.
3. For example, an area just behind your right ear enables you to perceive faces. Damage to this area can result in prosopagnosia, a disorder that causes an inability to detect differences in faces. Persons suffering from prosopagnosia cannot recognize their own face in a mirror.

VIII. GESTALT PRINCIPLES OF ORGANIZATION

A. INTRODUCTION

1. The German psychologist Max Wertheimer founded Gestalt psychology in the early 1900s.
2. Gestalt psychologists maintained that we actively process our sensations according to consistent perceptual rules. These rules create whole perceptions, or *gestalts*, that are meaningful, symmetrical, and as simple as conditions will allow.

B. THE FIGURE-GROUND RELATIONSHIP

1. The human tendency to distinguish between figure and ground is the most fundamental Gestalt principle or organization.
2. The figure is the main element of a scene that clearly stands out. In contrast, the ground is the less distinct background of a scene.
3. For example, the page you are now reading consists of lines of black markings on a white page. Your brain organizes these black markings into letters and groups them into words and sentences. The letters constitute the figure while the white page is the ground.

C. PERCEPTUAL GROUPING

1. The law of similarity
   ▸ *States that there is a tendency to perceive objects of a similar size, shape, or color as a unit or figure.*
   ▸ *For example, the crowd at a football game includes a wide assortment of different people. If you are following the law of similarity, you could perceptually organize the crowd into home fans, visiting fans, band members, and cheerleaders.*
2. The law of proximity
   ▸ *States that there is a tendency to perceive objects that are physically close to one another as a single unit.*

> ▸ For example, home fans and visiting fans usually group
> themselves on opposing sides of the stadium. Based
> upon the law of proximity, you would perceptually group
> the visiting fans into a single homogeneous group.

3. The law of closure
> ▸ States that there is a tendency to fill in the gaps in an
> incomplete image.
> ▸ For example, scoreboards always have headings labeled
> HOME and VISITORS. If your scoreboard said HO E and
> VISI ORS, you would fill in the missing letters M and T
> and thus complete the words.

IX. DEPTH PERCEPTION

A. INTRODUCTION

1. Depth perception is the ability to perceive three-dimensional
    space and to accurately judge distance.
2. Although it is possible to use sound and even smell to judge
    distances, we rely heavily on vision to perceive both distance
    and three-dimensional space.

B. THE "VISUAL CLIFF" EXPERIMENT

1. In a famous experiment, Eleanor Gibson placed infants
    old enough to crawl on a Plexiglas-topped table. On one
    side, Gibson placed a sheet of high-contrast red-and-white-
    checkered cloth flush against the underside of the glass. This
    gave both the appearance and the reality of a solid surface.
    On the other side, she placed a sheet of the same material
    four feet below the glass. This created the illusion of a "deep
    end" with a "visual cliff."
2. The infants almost always refused to venture beyond the
    shallow side of the visual cliff. They turned away from the
    "deep end" even when their mothers held a spinning toy and
    beckoned encouragingly for them to crawl forward.
3. The visual cliff experiment supports the conclusion that depth
    perception in humans is an innate capacity that emerges
    during infancy.

C. MONOCULAR DEPTH CUES

1. Require the use of only one eye to process distance or depth cues.

2. Linear perspective
   ‣ *Parallel lines appear to converge toward a vanishing point as they recede into the distance.*
   ‣ *See* The Annunciation *by Carlo Crivelli and* The Avenue *by Meindert Hobbema for famous paintings that use linear perspective.*

3. Aerial perspective
   ‣ *Distance objects often appear hazy and blurred compared to close objects.*
   ‣ *See* The Virgin of the Rocks *by Leonardo da Vinci and* The Harvesters *by Pieter Bruegel the Elder for famous paintings that use aerial perspective.*

4. Relative size
   ‣ *If two or more objects are assumed to be similar in size, the object that appears larger is perceived as being closer.*
   ‣ *See* Sunday Afternoon on the Island of La Grande Jatte *by George Seurat for a famous painting that illustrates relative size.*

5. Motion parallax
   ‣ *As you move, you use the speed of passing objects to estimate the distance of the objects.*
   ‣ *For example, when you are driving on an interstate highway, nearby telephone poles, fences, and roadside signs seem to zip by faster than distant hills.*

D. BINOCULAR DEPTH CUES

1. Require the use of both eyes to process distance or depth cues.

2. Convergence
   ‣ *Binocular depth cue in which the closer the object, the more the eyes converge, or turn inward.*

3. Retinal disparity
   ‣ *Binocular depth cue in which the separation of the eyes causes different images to fall on each retina.*

▶ When two retinal images are very different, we interpret the object as being close by. When two retinal images are more nearly identical, the object is perceived as being farther away.

▶ A person with only one eye lacks retinal disparity and would have difficulty climbing an irregular set of stairs.

Many students find retinal disparity a difficult concept to grasp. Don't spend valuable study time trying to master the scientific principles of how retinal disparity works. For purposes of the AP Psychology exam the key point is to know that retinal disparity is a binocular clue for depth perception.

States of Consciousness

I. UNDERSTANDING CONSCIOUSNESS

A. KEY DEFINITIONS

1. Consciousness is the personal awareness of thoughts, sensations, memories, and the external world.
2. William James likened consciousness to an ever-changing "stream" or "river" that nonetheless is perceived as unified and unbroken.

B. LEVELS OF AWARENESS

1. Controlled processes
   ‣ *Require focused, maximum attention, i.e., writing an SAT or ACT essay*
2. Automatic processes
   ‣ *Require minimal attention, i.e., walking in the mall while talking on a cell phone*
3. Subconscious
   ‣ *Below conscious awareness*
   ‣ *Sleeping and dreaming*
4. No awareness
   ‣ *Biologically-based lowest level of awareness*
   ‣ *Being in a coma or under anesthesia*

C. CIRCADIAN RHYTHMS

1. Biological processes that systematically vary over a period of about 24 hours.
2. Researchers have identified more than 100 bodily processes that rhythmically peak and dip each day. For example, our

sleep-wake cycle, blood pressure, secretion of different hormones, and pulse rate all follow circadian rhythms.

3. When all time cues are removed, our sleep-wake cycle averages about 25 hours.

4. Jet lag and rotating work schedules are common examples of activities that disrupt normal circadian rhythms. These disruptions can lead to reduced concentration and increased fatigue.

II. SLEEP PATTERNS

A. STUDYING SLEEP

1. Sleep researchers use an electroencephalograph to detect and record brain-wave changes during the sleep cycle.

2. Electroencephalogram (EEG) recordings show that sleep consists of a repeating pattern of distinct stages.

B. TWO BASIC TYPES OF SLEEP

1. REM or rapid-eye-movement sleep
   ▶ *Active sleep in which the sleeper's eyes dart back and forth behind closed eyelids*
   ▶ *Associated with dreaming*
2. NREM or non-rapid-eye-movement sleep
   ▶ *Quiet sleep*
   ▶ *Associated with slowing brain activity*
   ▶ *Divided into four stages*

C. STAGES OF NREM SLEEP

1. Stage 1
   ▶ *Period of light sleep that typically lasts only a few minutes*
   ▶ *Characterized by a slowing heart rate and decreasing blood pressure*
2. Stage 2
   ▶ *Period of true sleep that typically lasts 15 to 20 minutes*

> ▸ *Characterized by the periodic appearance of short bursts of rapid, high-amplitude brain waves known as sleep spindles.*

3. Stages 3 and 4
   > ▸ *Periods of deep sleep that typically last 20 to 40 minutes*
   > ▸ *Characterized by low levels of breathing, blood pressure, and heart rate*

D. REM SLEEP

1. The initial four NREM stages typically last about an hour.
2. After completing Stage 4, the sleeper reverses back through Stages 3 and 2. However, instead of reentering Stage 1, the sleeper enters REM sleep.
3. REM sleep is often referred to as "paradoxical sleep." A paradox is a phenomenon that is contradictory, but nonetheless true. REM sleep is paradoxical because it is simultaneously characterized by active eye movements and the loss of muscle movement. The suppression of voluntary muscle activity prevents the sleeper from acting out dreams.
4. The amount of REM sleep changes during our life span. Infants spend about 40 percent of their sleep in REM. This figure declines to 20 percent for adults and to 14 percent for people over 70.

E. SLEEP CYCLES

1. In a typical night, a sleeping person experiences five 90-minute cycles of alternating NREM and REM sleep.
2. The first REM episode is short. However, as the night progresses, the REM phases become longer and less time is spent in NREM.

Test Tip

Sleep cycles typically generate one or two very specific multiple-choice questions. Be sure you know that REM sleep is highly correlated with dreams and that sleep spindles occur in Stage 2 sleep.

KEY CONTENT REVIEW

III. THEORIES OF SLEEP

A. THE RESTORATION THEORY OF SLEEP

1. Proponents of this theory argue that sleep rejuvenates the mind and the body.
2. REM sleep restores mental and brain functions, while NREM sleep restores key physical functions.
3. The restoration theory is supported by studies in which researchers selectively deprive subjects of REM sleep. When subjects are allowed to resume uninterrupted sleep cycles, they experience a REM rebound or dramatic increase in REM sleep. The same rebound phenomenon occurs when subjects are deprived of NREM sleep.

B. THE ADAPTIVE THEORY OF SLEEP

1. Evolutionary psychologists argue that sleep patterns evolved so that both human and non-human animals could conserve energy and avoid predators.
2. Evolutionary psychologists also argue that sleep is a necessary part of circadian cycles.

IV. THEORIES OF DREAMS

A. THE PSYCHOANALYTIC/PSYCHODYNAMIC VIEW

1. In *The Interpretation of Dreams*, Freud boldly declared that dreams are "the royal road to the unconscious." According to Freud, dreams provide insights into unconscious motives by expressing hidden desires and conflicts.
2. According to Freud, dreams contain a story line or manifest content that consists of symbols.
3. The manifest symbols disguise the dream's true meaning. Freud believed that the latent or hidden content provides the dream's real unconscious meaning.
4. Although very provocative, Freud's theory is subjective and lacks scientific support.

B. THE ACTIVATION-SYNTHESIS VIEW

1. Sleep researcher J. Allan Hobson's research findings led him to propose that the dreaming brain is responding to its own internally generated signals.
2. The brain, Hobson argues, synthesizes these spontaneous signals into coherent patterns or dreams.
3. Hobson does not believe that dreams are completely meaningless. Unlike Freud, he believes that a dream's meaning is not derived from decoding hidden symbols, but from analyzing the personal way in which a dream organizes images.

V. SLEEP DISORDERS

A. INSOMNIA

1. The most common sleep disorder
2. Characterized by persistent problems in falling asleep, staying asleep, or awakening too early

B. SLEEP APNEA

1. Common in overweight men over the age of 50
2. Characterized by loud snoring, irregular breathing, and gasping for air

C. SLEEPWALKING

1. Sleepwalking is much more common in children than adults.
2. Characterized by an episode of walking or performing other actions during Stage 3 or Stage 4 of NREM sleep

D. NARCOLEPSY

1. Characterized by chronic sleep attacks which can occur at any time, in any place, and often at inappropriate times that may be accompanied by muscle paralysis.
2. The exact cause is unknown but it does appear to be genetic.

3. Treatment may involve medications including stimulants and antidepressants and utilizing scheduled naps.

 VI. HYPNOSIS

A. DEFINITION

1. Hypnosis is a trance-like state of heightened suggestibility, deep relaxation, and intense focus.

B. PRACTICAL APPLICATIONS

1. Used to reduce stress and anxiety
2. Used to treat chronic pain
3. Used to manage pain during medical and dental procedures
4. Used in efforts to lose weight and stop smoking

C. LIMITATIONS

1. No one can be hypnotized against his or her will.
2. Hypnosis cannot make people violate their moral values.
3. Hypnosis cannot bestow new talents or make a person stronger.

D. EXPLANATIONS OF HYPNOSIS

1. Dissociation

   ▸ *Ernest Hilgard conducted an experiment in which hypnotized subjects showed no sign of pain when they submerged their arms in an ice bath. However, when Hilgard asked the subjects to lift their index finger if they felt pain, 70 percent did.*

   ▸ *Hilgard theorized that hypnosis induces a special state of dissociation, or divided consciousness. Dissociation enables the hypnotized subjects to consciously respond to the hypnotist's suggestion that the cold water is not painful. At the same time, the hypnotized subjects processed a second dissociated stream of mental activity that enabled them to sense the water's temperature.*

2. Social influence theory

> ▸ *Proponents of the social influence theory argue that there is no such thing as a hypnotic trance. Instead, people are enacting the socially constructed role of hypnotic subject.*
>
> ▸ *The social influence theory explains Hilgard's findings by theorizing that his subjects ignored the cold because they were caught up in the role of being a hypnotized subject.*

> *Given the amount of attention devoted to Freud's psychoanalytic theory of dreams, it is easy to overlook the research of Ernest Hilgard on hypnosis. Don't make this mistake. Be sure that you can identify and briefly explain Hilgard's theory of dissociation.*

VII. PSYCHOACTIVE DRUGS

A. KEY TERMS

1. Psychoactive drugs—chemicals that change conscious awareness, mood, and/or perception.
2. Agonistic drugs—enhance a neurotransmitter's effect
3. Antagonistic drugs—inhibit a neurotransmitter's effect
4. Withdrawal—the painful experience associated with stopping the use of addictive drugs
5. Tolerance—bodily adjustment to higher and higher levels of a drug, which leads to decreased sensitivity.

B. DEPRESSANTS

1. Act on the brain and other parts of the central nervous system by decreasing bodily processes, reducing reaction times, and causing a feeling of well being.
2. Alcohol, barbiturates, and anti-anxiety drugs, such as Valium, are all depressants.
3. Alcohol is the most used and most abused depressant. Note that, regardless of the dose, alcohol is always a depressant.

4. The psychological effects of alcohol are strongly influenced by the user's expectations. As noted by David Myers, "When people believe that alcohol affects social behavior in certain ways, and believe, rightly or wrongly, that they have been drinking alcohol, they will behave accordingly."

C. STIMULANTS

1. Act on the brain and other parts of the central nervous system by producing alertness, excitement, elevated mood, and general responsiveness.
2. Caffeine, nicotine, amphetamine, and cocaine are all stimulants.
3. Each year, over 400,000 Americans die from smoking-related illnesses. Smoking plays a role in causing bronchitis, emphysema, and heart disease.
4. Cocaine is a highly addictive and particularly dangerous stimulant.

D. OPIATES

1. Numb the senses and relieve pain.
2. Morphine, heroine, and codeine are all opiates.
3. Opiates are extremely addictive and withdrawal is excruciatingly painful.

E. HALLUCINOGENS

1. Produce sensory or perceptual distortions called hallucinations.
2. Marijuana and LSD are the best-known hallucinogens.

Test Tip

Psychoactive drugs are a fascinating, timely, and controversial topic. While they are a significant public issue, proactive drugs play a limited role on the AP Psychology exam. Alcohol is the substance most frequently asked about on the AP Psychology exam. Be sure you know that it is a depressant and that its psychological effects are strongly influenced by the user's expectations.

Learning

I. INTRODUCTION

A. LEARNING

1. A lasting change in behavior or mental processes as the result of an experience.
2. Also note that while behavior can be observed, mental processes are much more difficult to study.

B. INSTINCTS VERSUS LEARNING

1. Instincts are unlearned behaviors due to evolutionary programming that are found in almost all members of a species. For example, bears hibernate, geese migrate, and salmon swim upstream to spawn.
2. Learning represents a significant evolutionary advance over instinctive behavior. Learning enables humans to acquire new knowledge that can be transferred from one generation to another.

II. CLASSICAL CONDITIONING

A. IVAN PAVLOV (1849–1936)

1. Ivan Pavlov was a Russian (and later Soviet) physiologist who was awarded a Nobel Prize in 1904 for his research on the digestive system of dogs.
2. While conducting experiments, Pavlov noticed that his dogs tended to salivate before food was actually delivered to their

mouths. Pavlov devoted three decades and 532 carefully designed experiments to studying the principles of classical conditioning.

3. The learning processes that Pavlov discovered are called classical conditioning because they were the first to be extensively studied in psychology.

B. FIVE COMPONENTS OF CLASSICAL CONDITIONING

1. Unconditioned stimulus (UCS)
   ▸ *A natural stimulus that reflexively elicits a response without the need for prior learning.*
   ▸ *Pavlov used food as the unconditioned stimulus because it produced a naturally occurring salivation reflex.*
   ▸ *Remember that the word "condition" means "learned." Thus, an unconditioned stimulus is really an "unlearned stimulus."*

2. Unconditioned response (UCR)
   ▸ *An unlearned response that is elicited by an unconditioned stimulus.*
   ▸ *In Pavlov's experiments, salivation was the unconditioned response.*

3. Neutral stimulus (NS)
   ▸ *Any stimulus that produces no conditioned response prior to learning.*
   ▸ *In Pavlov's experiments a ringing bell was originally a neutral stimulus.*

4. Conditioned stimulus (CS)
   ▸ *The conditioned stimulus was originally the neutral stimulus. When systematically paired with the unconditioned stimulus, the neutral stimulus becomes a conditioned (or learned) stimulus as it gains the power to cause a response.*
   ▸ *In Pavlov's experiments, the ringing bell became a conditioned stimulus when it began to produce the same salivating response that the food once produced.*

5. Conditioned response (CR)
   ▸ *A conditioned response is a learned response elicited by the conditioned stimulus.*
   ▸ *Pavlov called the process by which a conditioned stimulus elicits a conditioned response "acquisition."*

▸ *In Pavlov's experiments, he paired the ringing bell with food. Originally a neutral stimulus, the ringing bell became a conditioned stimulus when the dog reacted with a conditioned response by salivating. The dog thus formed a new, learned association between a ringing bell and the food.*

▸ *In Pavlov's experiments, the dog's salivation was both an unconditioned response and a conditioned response.*

▸ *Classical conditioning is most efficient when the conditioned stimulus immediately precedes the unconditioned stimulus.*

6. Example

▸ *Every time someone flushes a toilet in a health club locker room, the nearby shower becomes hot. The sudden stream of hot water causes the person taking a nearby shower to jump back. Over time, the person hears the flush and then automatically jumps back before the water temperature changes.*

▸ *In this example, the hot water is the unconditioned stimulus and jumping back is the unconditioned (and thus automatic) response. The toilet flush was originally a neutral stimulus that when paired with the hot water became a conditioned stimulus. The flushing sound thus elicits the conditioned response of jumping back before the hot water appears.*

C. EXTINCTION AND SPONTANEOUS RECOVERY

1. Extinction is the gradual weakening of a conditioned behavior when the conditioned stimulus is not followed by the unconditioned stimulus. For example, in Pavlov's experiments he presented the ringing bell without the food. As a result, the ringing bell gradually lost its power to elicit the conditioned response of salivation.

2. Spontaneous recovery is the reappearance of an extinguished conditioned response after a time delay. For example, Pavlov discovered that after a period of time, his dogs began salivating when they heard the sound of the bell. Note that the conditioned response reappeared at a lower intensity.

3. Spontaneous recovery shows how difficult it can be to eliminate a conditioned response. The noted psychologist

Philip Zimbardo points out that "extinction merely suppresses the conditioned response. What actually seems to be happening during extinction is the learning of a competing response *not to respond* to the conditioned stimulus."

D. STIMULUS GENERALIZATION AND DISCRIMINATION

1. Stimulus generalization
   ▸ *Occurs when stimuli that are similar to the original stimulus also elicit the conditioned response. It is important to remember that the new stimulus was not paired with the unconditioned stimulus.*
   ▸ *For example, Pavlov found that a dog conditioned to a low-pitched tone would also respond to a high-pitched tone.*

2. Stimulus discrimination
   ▸ *The ability to distinguish between two similar stimuli.*
   ▸ *For example, students have learned different responses to the sound of bells in classrooms, cell phones, and front doors. Similarly, gardeners demonstrate stimulus discrimination when they respond differently to weeds and to flowers.*

3. Example
   ▸ *A young boy demonstrates stimulus generalization when he is bitten by a neighbor's boxer and then becomes afraid and runs away when he sees any neighborhood dog.*
   ▸ *The same boy demonstrates stimulus discrimination if he still enjoys playing with his own family's pet collie.*

E. HIGHER-ORDER CONDITIONING

1. Higher-order conditioning or second-order conditioning occurs when a conditioned stimulus from one learning trial is paired with a new unconditioned stimulus. The new unconditioned stimulus becomes a new conditioned stimulus capable of eliciting the conditioned response even though it has never been paired with the unconditioned stimulus.

2. For example, Pavlov classically conditioned a dog to salivate to the sound of a ticking metronome. He then paired the ticking metronome with a black square. After several pairings of the ticking metronome and the black square, the black square produced salivation even though it had never been directly paired with food.

F. TASTE AVERSION AND CLASSICAL CONDITIONING

1. A classically conditioned dislike for and avoidance of a particular food that develops when an organism becomes ill after eating the food.

2. Many people have experienced vivid examples of taste aversion. For example, suppose you eat a pizza with a particularly spicy topping and then become ill with the flu. You then develop a dislike for the spicy topping and feel nauseated whenever you smell it. In this example, the flu sickness is the unconditioned stimulus and nausea is the unconditioned response. The spicy pizza topping is the conditioned stimulus and the nausea to the new food is the conditioned response.

3. While anecdotal examples are entertaining, they do not demonstrate a scientific cause-and-effect relationship. Psychologist John Garcia (b. 1917) conducted a series of controlled experiments to demonstrate that taste aversions could be produced in laboratory rats. In his basic experimental condition, Garcia first allowed rats to drink saccharin-flavored water (the neutral stimulus). A few hours later, he injected the rats with a drug (the unconditioned stimulus) that produced gastrointestinal distress (the unconditioned response). After recovering from the illness, the rats refused to drink the flavored water. Garcia concluded that the rats developed a taste aversion to the saccharin-flavored water.

4. Garcia's experiments challenged two basic principles of classical conditioning. First, the conditioning only required a single pairing. And second, instead of being separated by a few seconds, Garcia separated the two stimuli by several hours. Garcia's research thus demonstrated that there are important biological constraints on conditioning.

III. OPERANT CONDITIONING: INTRODUCTION

A. LIMITATIONS OF CLASSICAL CONDITIONING

1. Classical conditioning focuses on existing reflexive behaviors that are automatically elicited by a specific stimulus.
2. Learning, however, involves new behaviors or voluntary actions that classical conditioning cannot explain.

B. EDWARD L. THORNDIKE (1874–1949) AND THE LAW OF EFFECT

1. Animal behavior fascinated Edward L. Thorndike. His studies of baby chicks and cats were the first systematic investigations of animal learning.
2. Thorndike focused on how voluntary behaviors are influenced by their consequences. In his famous law of effect, Thorndike postulated that responses that lead to satisfying outcomes are more likely to be repeated. Similarly, responses followed by unpleasant outcomes are less likely to be repeated.

C. B.F. SKINNER (1904–1990) AND OPERANT CONDITIONING

1. B.F. Skinner was a renowned behaviorist who believed that psychologists should focus on observable behavior that could be objectively measured and verified.
2. During his long career, Skinner formulated the principles of operant conditioning. Skinner defined the term "operant" as any "active behavior that operates upon the environment to generate consequences." Operant conditioning is a learning process in which behavior is shaped and maintained by consequences (rewards or punishments) that follow a

response. In contrast, in classical conditioning behavior is controlled by the stimuli that precede a response.

IV. OPERANT CONDITIONING: REINFORCEMENT

A. BASIC DEFINITION OF REINFORCEMENT

1. Reinforcement occurs when a stimulus (the reinforcer) follows an active behavior or response.
2. The reinforcer increases the probability that the behavior or response will be repeated.

B. POSITIVE REINFORCEMENT

1. Definition
   ▸ *A situation in which a behavior or response is followed by the addition of a reinforcing stimulus. The stimulus increases the probability that the response will occur again.*
   ▸ *It is very important to understand that* positive *does not mean "good" or "desirable." Instead, Skinner used* positive *like a plus sign (+) to indicate that a response is strengthened because something is added.*

2. Examples
   ▸ *Your performance in the school play is flawless (the operant). Your drama coach applauds and exclaims "Bravo!" (the reinforcing stimulus).*
   ▸ *You make a special effort to help customers find the electronic products that will work best for them (the operant). Your boss gives you a raise to reward your hard work (the reinforcing stimulus).*
   ▸ *You earn an A on your AP Psychology mid-term exam (the operant). Your teacher writes you an outstanding letter of recommendation (the reinforcing stimulus).*

C. NEGATIVE REINFORCEMENT

1. Definition
   ▸ *A situation in which a behavior or response is followed by the removal of an adverse stimulus.*

> ‣ *It is very important to understand that* negative *does not mean "bad" or "undesirable." Instead, Skinner used* negative *like a minus sign (-) to indicate that a response is strengthened because something is subtracted or removed.*
> ‣ *Negative reinforcement typically enables you to either escape an existing aversive stimulus or avoid an aversive stimulus before it occurs.*

2. Examples

> ‣ *You take out the garbage (the operant) to avoid your mother's repeated nagging (the aversive stimulus).*
> ‣ *You put on sunscreen (the operant) to avoid getting sunburned (the aversive stimulus).*
> ‣ *You give your little brother a candy bar (the operant) to prevent him from crying (the aversive stimulus).*
> ‣ *Your little sister is crying (the operant). You hug her and she stops crying (the aversive stimulus).*

Test Tip

The AP Psychology Development Committee includes experienced classroom teachers who know that students easily understand positive reinforcement but have difficulty grasping negative reinforcement. As a result, AP Psychology exams usually have multiple-choice questions devoted to negative reinforcement. Remember, negative reinforcement increases the likelihood of a behavior by enabling you to either escape an existing aversive stimulus or avoid an aversive stimulus before it occurs.

D. THE PREMACK PRINCIPLE

1. Named after psychologist David Premack, the Premack principle states that the opportunity to engage in a preferred activity can be used to reinforce a less-preferred activity.

2. Examples

> ‣ *You enjoy playing video games far more than studying for the SAT or ACT. Knowing this, you tie the less-preferred activity (studying for the SAT or ACT) to your preferred activity (playing video games).*

▸ *You enjoy eating ice cream for dessert far more than eating vegetables. Knowing this, your mother ties the less-desired activity (eating vegetables) to your preferred activity (eating ice cream).*

E. TYPES OF REINFORCERS

1. Primary reinforcers
   - ▸ *A reinforcer that is naturally reinforcing for a given species.*
   - ▸ *Food, water, shelter, and sexual contact are all primary reinforcers.*

2. Secondary reinforcers
   - ▸ *A reinforcer that gains its effectiveness by a learned association with primary reinforcers.*
   - ▸ *Money is the most widely used secondary reinforcer in human societies.*

3. Token economy
   - ▸ *A therapeutic method, based on operant conditioning, by which individuals are rewarded with tokens that act as secondary reinforcers. The tokens can be redeemed for rewards and privileges.*
   - ▸ *Elementary teachers often use token economies as a reinforcement strategy. The token economy enables a teacher to reinforce classroom rules without having to know a specific reinforcer for each student.*

F. CONTINUOUS REINFORCEMENT AND SHAPING

1. Continuous reinforcement
   - ▸ *A reinforcement schedule in which all correct responses are reinforced.*
   - ▸ *Responses extinguish faster when they are learned through a continuous reinforcement schedule.*

2. Shaping
   - ▸ *The technique of strengthening behavior by reinforcing successive approximations of a behavior until the entire correct routine is displayed.*
   - ▸ *Shaping is extensively used by athletic coaches and animal trainers.*

G. INTERMITTENT REINFORCEMENT

1. The rewarding of some, but not all, correct responses.
2. Advantages
   ▸ *Intermittent reinforcement is the most efficient way to maintain behaviors that have already been learned.*
   ▸ *Behaviors learned through intermittent reinforcement are very resistant to extinction. As a result, gambling is a very difficult habit to extinguish.*

H. RATIO SCHEDULES OF REINFORCEMENT

1. Ratio schedules are based upon the number of responses.
2. Fixed ratio schedules
   ▸ *Reinforcement occurs after a predetermined set of responses.*
   ▸ *An employer who pays workers for every three baskets of fruit they pick is using a fixed ratio schedule.*
   ▸ *Fixed ratio schedules produce high response rates. However, there is a brief drop-off just after reinforcement.*
3. Variable ratio schedules
   ▸ *Reinforcement is unpredictable because the ratio varies.*
   ▸ *Casino owners use slot machines designed to operate on a variable ratio schedule.*
   ▸ *Variable ratio schedules produce high response rates and are very resistant to extinction.*

I. INTERVAL SCHEDULES OF REINFORCEMENT

1. Interval schedules are based on responses made within a certain time period.
2. Fixed interval schedules
   ▸ *Reinforcement occurs after a predetermined time has elapsed.*
   ▸ *Employers who pay their workers every two weeks are using a fixed interval schedule of reinforcement. Teachers who give a test every two weeks are also using a fixed interval schedule.*
   ▸ *Fixed interval schedules typically produce moderate response rates followed by a flurry of activity near the end of each interval.*

3. Variable interval schedules
   ‣ *Reinforcement occurs unpredictably since the time interval varies.*
   ‣ *Teachers who give pop quizzes are using a variable interval schedule.*
   ‣ *Variable interval schedules produce low but steady response rates because respondents cannot predict when they will be rewarded.*

V. OPERANT CONDITIONING: PUNISHMENT

A. DEFINITION

1. Punishment is a process in which a behavior is followed by an aversive consequence that decreases the likelihood of the behavior being repeated.
2. Do not confuse punishment and reinforcement. Punishment decreases the likelihood of a behavior being repeated, while reinforcement increases the likelihood that the behavior will be repeated.

B. POSITIVE PUNISHMENT

1. The application or adding of an aversive stimulus after a response.
2. Examples
   ‣ *You arrive late to work (the operant) and are reprimanded by your supervisor (the aversive stimulus).*
   ‣ *You show off your knowledge of a subject by answering all of your teacher's questions (the operant) and a popular girl makes a snide remark about you (the aversive stimulus).*

C. NEGATIVE PUNISHMENT

1. The removal or subtraction of a reinforcing stimulus.
2. Negative punishment and negative reinforcement are easily confused. However, it is important to keep in mind that they are very different. Negative punishment makes a behavior less

likely to happen. In contrast, negative reinforcement makes a behavior more likely to happen.

3. Examples
    ▸ *You arrive at work late (the operant) and are sent home without pay (the loss of a reinforcing stimulus).*
    ▸ *You show off your knowledge of a subject by answering all your teacher's questions (the operant) and a popular girl doesn't invite you to her party (the loss of a reinforcing stimulus).*

D. DRAWBACKS OF PUNISHMENT

1. Punishment can produce undesirable results such as fear, hostility, and aggression.
2. Punishment often produces only a temporary change in behavior.
3. Punishment can produce a behavior pattern called learned helplessness. This occurs when a learner feels that it is impossible to escape punishment. This leads to a passive feeling of hopelessness that may lead to depression. For example, a student who is doing poorly in a difficult course may express a sense of learned hopelessness by saying, "No matter what I do I'm going to fail."

E. EFFECTIVE USES OF PUNISHMENT

1. Punishment should be delivered immediately after the offensive behavior.
2. Punishment should be certain.
3. Punishment should be limited and sufficient so that it "fits the crime."
4. Punishment should focus on the behavior, not the character, of the offender.

VI. COMPARING CLASSICAL CONDITIONING AND OPERANT CONDITIONING

A. PIONEERS

1. Classical conditioning—Ivan Pavlov and John B. Watson
2. Operant conditioning—Edward Thorndike and B.F. Skinner

B. TYPES OF BEHAVIOR

1. Classical conditioning—involuntary responses
2. Operant conditioning—voluntary responses

C. TIMING OF STIMULI

1. Classical conditioning—stimuli precede the response
2. Operant conditioning—stimuli follow the response

D. USE OF REWARDS AND PUNISHMENTS

1. Classical conditioning—does not use rewards and punishments
2. Operant conditioning—based upon rewards and punishments

 VII. COGNITIVE PROCESSES

A. THE LIMITATIONS OF BEHAVIORIST THEORIES OF LEARNING

1. Behaviorists believe that classical and operant conditioning explain almost all learning.
2. However, cognitive psychologists believe that the behaviorists underestimate the importance of cognitive processes. They argue that cognitive or mental processes such as thinking and perception also play a key role in learning.

B. WOLFGANG KOHLER'S (1887–1967) STUDY OF INSIGHT

1. In a pioneering series of experiments Wolfgang Kohler suspended bananas just outside the reach of a caged chimpanzee named Sultan. Unlike Skinner's rats and pigeons,

KEY CONTENT REVIEW

Sultan did not solve the problem through trial-and-error. Instead, he studied the problem and in a flash of insight used a stick to knock down the fruit.

2. Kohler called this sudden understanding of a problem "insight learning." It is important to note that Sultan's behavior cannot be explained by either classical or operant conditioning.

C. EDWARD TOLMAN'S (1898–1956) STUDY OF LATENT LEARNING

1. In a classic study, Edward C. Tolman allowed one group of rats to run through a maze to obtain food. Tolman then allowed a second group of rats to explore the maze without receiving food. Some time later, Tolman compared the two groups to determine how quickly they could find the food at the end of the maze. Tolman reported that the second group of untrained rats found the food as quickly as the first group of trained rats.

2. Tolman explained his findings by hypothesizing that the untrained rats developed a cognitive map or mental representation of the maze. They then used this latent or hidden learning to rapidly find the food.

3. Remember that latent learning is not outwardly used until the situation calls for it.

VIII. OBSERVATIONAL LEARNING

A. DEFINITION

1. Observational learning occurs through watching others and then imitating or modeling the observed behavior.

2. Observational learning is also known as "social learning."

B. ALBERT BANDURA'S (B. 1925) CLASSIC BOBO DOLL STUDIES

1. Bandura and his colleagues allowed 4-year-old children to separately watch a live or televised adult model aggressively kick, punch, and shout at a large inflated Bobo doll. A second control group did not watch the aggressive models. Bandura

then allowed the children to play in a room with several toys, including a Bobo doll. The children who watched the live or televised aggressive model were much more likely to imitate the model's aggressive behavior than the children in the control group.

2. Bandura's experiment demonstrated the powerful influence of observational learning on behavior.

C. EXAMPLES

1. A high school basketball player attends a summer camp taught by college basketball players. The high school player returns home and incorporates some of their moves, trash talk, and training practices into his or her game.

2. Parents want to teach their five-year-old twins to share a bedroom. The parents model sharing behavior by demonstrating such cooperative behaviors as making the bed, hanging up clothes, and sweeping the floor.

Test Tip

Observational or social learning typically generates one multiple-choice question on each AP Psychology exam. However, in recent years observational learning has played a significant role in free-response questions. For example, both the 2002 and 2008 exams asked students to apply principles of observational learning to everyday situations.

Cognition

I. MEMORY

A. BASIC DEFINITION

1. Memory
   ▸ *Mental processes involved in acquiring, storing, and recovering knowledge.*
   ▸ *Memory creates an internal record of an experience.*

B. BASIC TASKS

1. Encoding–acquiring information into the memory system
2. Storage–retaining information over time
3. Retrieval–recovering information from memory storage

II. STAGE ONE–SENSORY MEMORY

A. FUNCTION

1. Everything that our senses hear, see, taste, touch, and smell enters our sensory memory.
2. Sensory memories give a sense of flow and continuity to experiences that would otherwise seem to be a confusing barrage of sounds, sights, tastes, textures, and odors.

B. CAPACITY AND DURATION

1. Sensory memory's capacity is large but not unlimited.
2. Sensory memory holds visual images for up to one-half second and auditory messages for up to 2 to 4 seconds.

C. TYPES

1. There is a sensory register for each sense.
2. Iconic memory records visual information.
3. Echoic memory records auditory information.

III. STAGE TWO–SHORT-TERM MEMORY

A. FUNCTION

1. The temporary storage site where sensory information is processed, evaluated, and analyzed. The information can be forgotten or added to long-term memory.
2. Short-term memory also accesses and retrieves information from long-term memory.

B. CAPACITY AND DURATION

1. Short-term memory has a limited capacity. Research indicates that the working capacity of short-term memory is typically seven pieces of information.
2. Short-term memory holds information for approximately 30 seconds.

C. EXTENDING THE CAPACITY AND DURATION OF SHORT-TERM MEMORY

1. Chunks and chunking
   - *A chunk is a single unit of information.*
   - *The capacity of short-term memory can be extended by grouping separate chunks of information into a new unit or chunk. For example, the four digits 2-0-1-0 can be combined to form the date 2010 and thus remembered as one chunk of information.*
2. Maintenance rehearsal
   - *Maintenance rehearsal is the process of repeating information to keep it in short-term memory.*
   - *Most students use maintenance rehearsal as a way of "cramming" information before a test. While*

maintenance rehearsal will keep information fresh in your short-term memory, it is not an efficient method of transferring information to your long-term memory.

▸ *Rehearsal is a vital process. Without rehearsal, information cannot be transferred to long-term memory.*

3. Elaborative rehearsal

▸ *The depth of processing determines how well information will be remembered.*

▸ *Elaborative rehearsal is a process by which new information is actively reviewed and related to information already stored in long-term memory. For example, a student trying to learn the SAT vocabulary word* vivacious *might try repeating the definition "full of life" over and over again. An alternative and much more effective strategy would be to relate the English word* vivacious *to the Spanish word* vivir, *"to live." This active process of elaborative rehearsal will greatly facilitate transferring the meaning of* vivacious *into long-term memory.*

▸ *Elaborative rehearsal has a number of advantages. It improves the organization of the material, encourages thinking about the meaning of the material, and increases connections between the material and prior knowledge.*

IV. LONG-TERM MEMORY

A. FUNCTION

1. Long-term memory serves as a storehouse of information.
2. When properly organized and integrated, information is readily available for retrieval.

B. CAPACITY AND DURATION

1. The capacity of long-term memory is unlimited.
2. The duration of long-term memory can be permanent.

C. PROCEDURAL MEMORY

1. Procedural memory includes motor skills, habits, and other memories of how things are done.
2. Remembering how to roller skate, ride a bicycle, and tie a shoe are all examples of procedural memory.
3. Procedural memory also includes classically conditioned responses to conditioned stimuli. For example, phobias and attitudes toward a variety of groups are part of procedural memory.

D. DECLARATIVE MEMORY

1. Episodic memory
   ▸ *A subdivision of declarative memory that stores memories of personal experiences and events.*
   ▸ *Episodic memories include your first romantic kiss, your "sweet sixteen" birthday party, and your first time taking the SAT or ACT.*
2. Semantic memory
   ▸ *A subdivision of declarative memory that stores memories of facts and general knowledge.*
   ▸ *Semantic memories include the Pythagorean theorem, the names of the three branches of government, and the functions of short-term memory.*

V. RETRIEVAL AND LONG-TERM MEMORY

A. THE SERIAL-POSITION EFFECT

1. The primacy effect–information from the beginning of a list is remembered better than material in the middle.
2. The recency effect–information from the end of a list is remembered better than material in the middle.
3. Examples
   ▸ *You remember the first and last people you meet at a party better than those you meet in-between.*
   ▸ *You remember America's first and last presidents better than those who served in the late 1800s.*

B. RETRIEVAL CUES

1. Recall
   - *The use of a general cue to retrieve a memory.*
   - *For example, your AP Psychology teacher asks you to write down everything you remember about yesterday's lesson on long-term memory without referring to your notes.*

2. Recognition
   - *The use of a specific cue to retrieve a memory.*
   - *For example, your language arts teacher asks you to define the term allusion by saying, "It's like in Taylor Swift's song 'Love Story' when she says, 'Cause you were Romeo, I was a scarlet letter.'"*

VI. FORGETTING

A. THE FORGETTING CURVE

1. Hermann Ebbinghaus (1850–1909) was a German psychologist who conducted pioneering research on forgetting.

2. Ebbinghaus invented three-letter nonsense syllables such as TIX and ZEL. He then tested his recall of them after varying amounts of time.

3. Ebbinghaus' famous forgetting curve shows two distinct patterns. First, memories of relatively meaningless information are lost shortly after they have been learned. Second, following this initial plunge, the rate of forgetting levels off and then slowly declines.

4. The Ebbinghaus forgetting curve can be applied to such common experiences as learning names at a party or cramming facts before an exam. Most of the names and facts are then quickly forgotten.

B. INTERFERENCE THEORY

1. According to the interference theory, forgetting takes place when one memory must compete with another similar memory. The similarity between the two memories creates interference and forgetting.

2. Proactive interference
   ▸ *Occurs when old information interferes with recalling new information.*
   ▸ *For example, you learn and perform a dance routine for your fall school play. You then experience trouble remembering a new dance routine for the winter play because of proactive interference from the prior fall routine.*

3. Retroactive interference
   ▸ *Occurs when new information interferes with recalling old information.*
   ▸ *For example, you learn how to drive on a car with a manual transmission ("stick shift"). Your parents then buy you a new car with an automatic transmission. On a family vacation, your parents rent a car with a "stick shift." You have trouble driving the rental car because of retroactive interference from driving your new automatic car.*

AP Psychology test writers know that students often confuse proactive and retroactive interference. Don't be confused. Proactive interference means that an old memory is moving forward ("pro") to interfere with a new memory. For example, your memory of the combination to your old locker reaches forward and interferes with remembering the combination to your new locker. Retroactive interference means that a new memory moves backward ("retro") to interfere with an old memory. For example, your team learns a new set of plays that now interfere with your performance of the old plays.

C. ENCODING FAILURE

1. Encoding failure occurs when poorly encoded information is passed from the short-term memory to the long-term memory.

2. As your teachers have no doubt repeated, paying attention is vital to retention. Your teachers are right. Divided attention is one of the most common causes of encoding failure. Studies show that when we try to perform multiple tasks, the information is not properly encoded into long-term memory.

3. For example, text-messaging a friend while parking your car at the mall. By dividing your attention between texting and parking, you created an encoding failure that might come back to haunt you a few hours later when you try to find your car.

D. RETRIEVAL FAILURE

1. An encoding failure takes place when information is not properly stored in long-term memory. In contrast, a retrieval failure takes place when information stored in long-term memory is available, but momentarily inaccessible.
2. Interference, faulty cues, and emotional states such as test anxiety, can all cause retrieval failure.
3. The "tip-of-the-tongue" phenomenon is a common example of retrieval failure. It describes the feeling that at any moment a name or place you are trying to remember is just out of reach but will soon pop out from the "tip of your tongue."

VII. AMNESIA

A. BASIC DEFINITION

1. Amnesia is a severe memory loss.

B. RETROGRADE AMNESIA

1. People who suffer from retrograde amnesia are unable to remember some or all of their past. Retrograde amnesia especially affects episodic memories for recent events.
2. Automobile and motorcycle accidents are leading causes of retrograde amnesia.
3. For example, on August 31, 1997, Diana, Princess of Wales, her companion Dodi Fayed, and driver Henri Paul were all killed in a car accident in Paris. Fayed's bodyguard, Trevor Rees-Jones, was the only survivor. Because of severe head injuries, Rees-Jones suffers from retrograde amnesia and cannot recall particulars of the accident.

C. ANTEROGRADE AMNESIA

1. People who suffer from anterograde amnesia are unable to form new memories.
2. The best-known and most extensively studied case of anterograde amnesia is that of Henry Molaison (1926–2008), better known as H.M.
3. H.M. suffered from severe epileptic seizures. In 1953, his surgeon removed portions of H.M.'s medial temporal lobes, including his hippocampus. The experimental surgery successfully controlled H.M.'s epilepsy. However, doctors soon discovered the H.M could not commit new events to long-term memory. Known as "The Man Who Couldn't Remember," H.M. lived in an eternal present.
4. Psychologists Brenda Milner and Suzanne Corkin worked with H.M. for over 30 years. Their exhaustive studies revolutionized understanding of the organization of human memory and helped establish the field of neuropsychology.

VIII. MEMORY DISTORTION

A. INTRODUCTION

1. The human memory is far from perfect. Important details can be changed, exaggerated, and even deleted.
2. Elizabeth Loftus (b. 1944) is an American psychologist who is a renowned expert on memory distortion.

B. THE MISINFORMATION EFFECT

1. A memory distortion phenomenon in which a person's existing memories can be altered if a person is exposed to misleading information.
2. In a classic study, Loftus showed her subjects a film of an automobile accident. The subjects recorded what they saw and answered a series of questions including, "About how fast were the cars going when they contacted each other?" Loftus then varied the question by substituting the verbs "hit," "bumped," "collided," and "smashed" for the word

"contacted." The choice of words significantly influenced the subjects' estimate of how fast the cars were traveling. For example, the word "contacted" elicited an average speed estimate of 32 miles per hour. In contrast, "smashed" produced an average speed estimate of 41 miles per hour.

3. Loftus' use of suggestive questions provides compelling evidence of how the information a person receives after an event can lead to memory distortion.

IX. STRATEGIES FOR MEMORY IMPROVEMENT

A. MNEMONICS

1. Strategies for improving memory.
2. The most effective mnemonic strategies make connections between new material and information already in long-term memory.

B. THE METHOD OF LOCI

1. First developed by ancient Greek and Roman orators to help them remember key points in their speeches.
2. In this technique, the speaker first memorizes the layout of a building, street, garden, or any geographic entity with a number of discrete loci (plural of Latin *locus* for place or location). The speaker then attaches key items to each place. The speaker retrieves the information by "walking" through the loci and allowing each place to cue the desired items.
3. For example, as part of an AP Psychology class project on memory, you need to give a brief oral report on the types of long-term memory. You might use the method of loci by attaching procedural memory to the bicycle in your garage, episodic memory to family pictures in the den, and semantic memory to the computer in your room.

C. ACRONYMS

1. The acronym method involves creating a code word from the first letters of the items you want to remember.

2. For example, Roy G. Biv is a well-known acronym for remembering the sequence of hues (red, orange, yellow, green, blue, indigo, and violet) in a rainbow or any visible spectrum.

X. LANGUAGE

A. DEFINITION

1. Language is a form of communication using spoken and written words and gestures that are combined according to specific rules.
2. Language allows us to communicate and preserve thoughts, ideas, feeling, and experiences.

B. BUILDING BLOCKS OF LANGUAGE

1. Phonemes
   ▸ *The smallest distinctive units of sound used in a language.*
   ▸ *English speakers use approximately 44 phonemes. For example, the p in "party" and the ng in "ping" are both phonemes.*
2. Morphemes
   ▸ *The smallest units of meaning in a language.*
   ▸ *Morphemes can be words, such as "I" and "a," or they can be parts of words such as the prefix un and the suffix able. For example, the word "unbreakable" consists of three morphemes—the prefix un, the root word break, and the suffix able.*

It is very easy to overlook phonemes and morphemes. Remember that a phoneme is the smallest unit of sound and a morpheme is the smallest unit of meaning. One mnemonic device for remembering these terms is to attach them to the familiar PM part of the day. The P comes before the M just as phonemes precede morphemes.

3. Syntax
   ▸ *Grammatical rules for putting words in correct order.*
   ▸ *Sentences are sequences of words constructed according to the rules of syntax. Each language has its own syntax.*
4. Overregulation of grammar rules
   ▸ *Overregulation occurs when children apply a grammatical rule too widely and therefore create incorrect forms.*
   ▸ *The following sentence by a three-year-old contains two examples of overregulation: "I holded the window closed, daddy, and now the mouses can't get out." Note that the child used "holded" instead of "held" and "mouses" instead of "mice."*

C. NOAM CHOMSKY (B. 1928) AND LANGUAGE DEVELOPMENT

1. Noam Chomsky is a renowned linguist who argues that young children possess an innate capacity to learn and produce speech.
2. Chomsky notes that children in widely different cultures progress through the same stages of language development at about the same ages.
3. Chomsky hypothesized that humans learn language because of innate speech-enabling structures called the language acquisition device or LAD.

D. BENJAMIN WHORF (1897–1941) AND THE EFFECT OF LANGUAGE ON THOUGHT

1. Benjamin Whorf was a linguist who believed that a language does more than describe a person's culture. Whorf argued that a person's language may also shape a person's thoughts and perceptions. This proposal is called the linguistic relativity hypothesis.
2. Whorf illustrated his hypothesis by pointing out that Eskimos (Inuits) have many different words for snow. In contrast, English has the one word—"snow." According to Whorf, "We have the same word for falling snow, snow on the ground, snow packed hard like ice, slushy snow, wind-driven flying

snow–whatever the situation may be. To an Eskimo, this all-inclusive word would be almost unthinkable; he would say that falling snow, slushy snow, and so on are sensuously and operationally different...he uses different words for them and for other kinds of snow."

3. Contemporary researchers now challenge Whorf's hypothesis. They point out that the English language contains a number of words to describe various forms of snow, including "sleet," "slush," and "powder."

4. Linguists now believe that language influences, but does not determine, thought.

XI. BUILDING BLOCKS OF THOUGHT

A. MENTAL IMAGES

1. A mental picture of a previously stored sensory experience.

2. Images can be visual, such as imagining what a rainbow looks like. However, images are not strictly limited to visual pictures. For example, you can probably create a mental representation for the sound of a roaring race car, the smell of barbecued chicken, or the feel of a warm breeze blowing through your hair.

B. CONCEPTS

1. A mental category formed to group objects, events, or situations that share similar features and characteristics.

2. Artificial or formal concepts are defined by a specific set of rules or features. Geometric shapes, such as triangles, squares, and rectangles, are all formal concepts.

3. Natural concepts are formed by everyday experience. Vehicles, birds, and fruit are all natural concepts.

4. A prototype is the most typical instance of a particular concept. For example, a car would be the prototypical example of a vehicle, a robin would be the prototypical example of a bird, and an apple would be the prototypical example of a fruit.

C. SCHEMAS AND SCRIPTS

1. A schema is an organized mental framework about a particular topic, event, object, idea, setting, or group of people. For example, to a student the word "high school" probably conjures up a schema that includes classrooms, cafeterias, science labs, band rooms, and athletic fields.

2. A script is a type of schema that involves the typical sequence of behavior expected at an everyday event. For example, we have scripts for riding a school bus, attending a class, going to a Christmas party, and taking a date to a movie.

3. Schemas play an important role in how we learn to categorize different groups of people. For example, children learn different schemas for racial groups that can include stereotypes and prejudices.

AP Psychology test writers have used the concept of schema in both multiple-choice and free-response questions. The multiple-choice questions typically focus on the definition of a schema as a mental construct built up through experience. The free-response questions ask you to apply the concept of schema to an everyday problem or social situation. For example, a 1995 free-response question asked students to explain how schemas contribute to the phenomena of prejudice.

XII. PROBLEM-SOLVING STRATEGIES

A. ALGORITHMS

1. An algorithm is a logical, step-by-step procedure that, if followed correctly, will eventually solve a specific problem.

2. Mathematical formulas are examples of algorithms. For example, the formula for computing the area of a triangle (1/2 base × height) is an algorithm.

B. HEURISTIC

1. A heuristic is a general rule of thumb or shortcut that is used to reduce the number of possible solutions.

2. High school students interested in attending college can visit all the possible choices (an algorithm). However, this strategy would be impractical. Instead, students use a heuristic by limiting their search to small liberal arts colleges located within 300 miles of their homes.

XIII. OBSTACLES TO SOLVING PROBLEMS

A. MENTAL SET

1. The tendency to continue using belief systems and problem-solving strategies that worked in the past.

2. President Hoover's response to the Great Depression illustrates how mental sets can be an obstacle to solving problems. Hoover's belief system emphasized rugged individualism, the importance of private charities, and a laissez-faire or "hands off" attitude toward government intervention in the economy. Because of this mental set, Hoover failed to adopt the new Keynesian economic model that stressed massive government spending programs to revive the economy.

B. FUNCTIONAL FIXEDNESS

1. The tendency to think of an object as functioning only in its usual or customary way. As a result, individuals often do not see unusual or innovative uses for familiar objects.

2. For example, Courtney and his wife Audrey are enjoying a visit to a tropical rainforest. One day while on a canoe trip a summer rainstorm suddenly approaches, catching them by surprise. They are soon soaked because they did not think of cutting holes in their environmentally friendly plastic trash bags and using them as improvised raincoats.

C. CONFIRMATION BIAS

1. A preference for information that confirms preexisting positions or beliefs, while ignoring or discounting contradictory evidence.

2. Christopher Columbus's famous voyage in 1492 provides one of history's best-known examples of a confirmation bias. Searching for a new water route to the Indies, Columbus in fact bumped into several Caribbean islands. Nonetheless, Columbus was so certain that he had reached the Indies that he called the native peoples Indians.

D. THE AVAILABILITY HEURISTIC

1. Judging the likelihood of an event based on readily available personal experiences or news reports.

2. Mega Millions is America's largest jackpot game with jackpots starting at $12 million and reaching up to $390 million. Mega Millions creates vivid memories by running TV commercials featuring ecstatic winners. By ignoring the millions of losers, the advertisements help create an unrealistic availability heuristic.

E. THE REPRESENTATIVE HEURISTIC

1. Judging the likelihood of an event based on how well it matches a typical example.

2. Kara is an attractive, fun-loving person who enjoys shopping, tanning at the beach, and attending rock concerts. When asked whether it is more likely that Kara is a model or an elementary school teacher, most respondents chose the former. In reality, there are far more female elementary school teachers than female models. The respondents' choice of a model illustrates the representative heuristic because the description of Kara matched their prototype of how a model should look and behave.

XIV. CREATIVITY

A. BASIC DEFINITION

1. Creativity is a mental process that produces novel solutions to problems.

B. DIVERGENT THINKING

1. A type of thinking in which problem solvers devise a number of possible alternative approaches. Divergent thinking is a major element in creativity.

2. The Great Depression tested the creativity of both President Hoover and President Roosevelt. Hoover failed to improve economic conditions because he was locked into a rigid mental set. In contrast, FDR embraced divergent thinking when he proposed a New Deal based upon "bold, persistent experimentation."

C. CHARACTERISTICS OF CREATIVE THINKING

1. Creative people are independent thinkers who resist social pressures to conform.

2. Creative people display a willingness to grow, change, and take risks.

3. Creative people are internally motivated and display an ability to focus their full attention on a problem.

4. Creative people are drawn to complex, challenging problems.

Motivation and Emotion

I. THEORIES OF MOTIVATION

A. INTRODUCTION

1. Motivation is the general term for the biological, emotional, cognitive, and social processes involved in starting, directing, and maintaining behavior.

2. Human behavior includes a wide range of motives and drives. No single comprehensive theory of motivation can explain the enormous variety of human behavior. As a result, psychologists have developed several theories of motivation.

B. INSTINCT THEORY

1. Instincts are fixed action patterns that are not learned and occur in most members of a species.

2. Animals display a number of fixed action patterns including bird migrations, mating rituals, and dominance displays.

3. Inspired by Darwin's theory of evolution, early psychologists, led by William James, listed scores of human instincts including modesty, cleanliness, rivalry, and parental love.

4. Instinct theory soon fell out of favor as it became evident that it lacked the ability to fully explain human motivation. Today, psychologists taking the evolutionary perspective explore the influence of our evolutionary history on eating, the selection of mates, the expression of emotions, and other patterns of human behavior.

C. DRIVE REDUCTION THEORY

1. The drive reduction theory replaced instinct theory during the 1930s.

2. The drive reduction theory is based on the biological concept of homeostasis. This key concept literally means "standing still." According to the principle of homeostasis, the body seeks to maintain a stable internal state, such as constant internal temperature and fluid levels. For example, after completing a marathon, runners drink a large quantity of water to restore homeostasis in their fluid levels.

3. The body creates a state of tension, known as a "drive," if any of its needs are unmet. For example, drive reduction theory states that a person will drink water as a result of a drive for satisfying thirst and eat food as a result of a drive for satisfying hunger.

4. The drive reduction theory is still used to explain motivated behaviors that have a clear biological basis. However, the drive reduction theory cannot account for many human behaviors. For example, buying the newest cell phone, contributing to a charity, and participating in an extreme sport cannot be explained by the satisfaction of a biological need.

D. AROUSAL THEORY

1. According to arousal theory, humans (and other animals) are innately curious and seek out complexity and novelty.

2. The Yerkes-Dodson law states that an optimal level of psychological arousal helps performances. When arousal is too low, our minds wander and we become bored. When arousal is too high, we become too anxious and "freeze-up." People are thus motivated to seek a moderate level of stimulation that is neither too easy nor too difficult.

3. For example, a youth soccer league proposes to implement a system in which games are played without keeping score. Removing scores may improve the performance of players who were too anxious. However, removing scores may cause highly competitive players to become bored, thus undermining their performance.

E. MASLOW'S HIERARCHY OF NEEDS

1. The humanist psychologist Abraham Maslow created a hierarchy of needs that combines and prioritizes biological, psychological, and social needs.

2. Maslow identified a progression of five needs. According to Maslow, people begin with basic physiological and safety needs. Once these needs are met, the individual "moves up" to high-level needs culminating with self-actualization.

3. Maslow's hierarchy of needs are as follows:
   - *Physiological needs: food, water, warmth, and maintenance of homeostasis*
   - *Safety needs: security, safety, and avoidance of pain*
   - *Belonging needs: acceptance, affection, and friendship*
   - *Esteem needs: feelings of accomplishment, approval, and recognition*
   - *Self-actualization needs: fulfilling one's potential by being all that you can be*

4. Psychologists have criticized Maslow's model for its vague definition of self-actualization. In addition, it is possible for people living in poverty to nonetheless develop strong social ties and self-esteem.

AP Psychology test writers have focused more attention on Maslow's hierarchy of needs than on instinct theory or drive reduction theory. You might use the initials PS BES as a mnemonic device to help you remember the sequence of Maslow's five needs. The "P" stands for Physiological, the "S" stands for Safety, the "B" stands for Belonging, the "E" stands for Esteem, and the "S" stands for Self-actualization.

II. HUNGER MOTIVATION

A. THE BIOLOGICAL BASIS OF HUNGER

1. The hypothalamus is a part of the forebrain structure that regulates eating and drinking.

2. When stimulated, the lateral hypothalamus (or hunger center) causes an animal to eat. If this area is destroyed, an animal will starve to death.

3. When stimulated, the ventromedial hypothalamus (the satiety center) causes the animal to stop eating. If this area is destroyed, the animal will eat constantly and gain more and more weight.

4. Set-point theory states that humans and other animals have a natural or optimal body-fat level. Like a thermostat, the body defends this set-point weight by regulating feelings of hunger and body metabolism.

B. OBESITY

1. Two-thirds of adult Americans are officially overweight, and about half of them are obese.

2. Obesity is not limited to adults. One in six Americans between the ages of 6 and 19 are overweight.

3. Obesity contributes to heart disease, diabetes, kidney failure, and many forms of cancer. About 300,000 adult deaths in the United States are directly attributable to obesity.

4. Factors involved in becoming overweight and obese:
   ▸ *Most Americans live in an environment with abundant and easily obtainable high-fat, high-calorie foods. As a result, during the last 20 years average daily caloric intake has increased nearly 10 percent for men and 7 percent for women.*
   ▸ *Many Americans lead a sedentary lifestyle. Nearly 4 out of 10 Americans report that they never exercise.*
   ▸ *Lack of adequate sleep increases the production of the appetite-increasing hormone ghrelin while decreasing production of the appetite-suppressing hormone leptin.*
   ▸ *Many people may be genetically predisposed to obesity. Studies reveal that people with a family history of obesity are two to three times more likely than people with no such history to become obese.*

C. ANOREXIA NERVOSA

1. Anorexia nervosa is an eating disorder characterized by a severe loss of weight resulting from self-imposed starvation and an obsessive fear of obesity.

2. The vast majority of anorexics are women.
3. Many psychologists believe that pervasive cultural images of the "thin ideal" of physical beauty create a distorted body image and a need for physical perfection.

D. BULIMIA NERVOSA

1. Bulimia nervosa is an eating disorder involving binge eating followed by vomiting, excessive exercise, or the use of laxatives.
2. Bulimia is difficult to initially detect because of weight fluctuations within or just above the normal range.
3. Bulimia causes cardiac arrhythmias, severe damage to the throat, and serious digestive disorders.

 III. SOCIAL MOTIVATION

A. ACHIEVEMENT MOTIVATION

1. The drive to succeed, especially in competition with others
2. Research studies by David McClelland (1917–1998) and others show that individuals with a high need for achievement (nAch) typically seek out tasks that are moderately difficult.
3. Achievement motivation is learned early in life, typically from parents. Highly motivated people are willing to work long hours, overcome obstacles, and delay gratification to focus on a goal.
4. Students display achievement motivation when they take several practice tests to hone skills for the SAT and ACT. A student with a high level of achievement motivation who scores a 2200 on the SAT and a 33 on the ACT would probably take the test again to achieve an even higher score.
5. Achievement motivation takes different forms in individualistic and collectivistic cultures. In individualistic cultures such as the United States, achievement motivation emphasizes personal success. In contrast, in collectivistic cultures such as China, achievement motivation emphasizes promoting the status or well-being of the family and other relevant social groups.

B. EXTRINSIC MOTIVATION

1. Based upon external rewards or threats of punishment

2. Students who work for grades, athletes who work for scholarships, and employees who work for bonuses are all motivated by external rewards. Athletes who work hard so they will not be benched are motivated by the threat of extrinsic punishment.

3. When extrinsic rewards and punishments are removed, behavior often falls to a lower level. For example, when seniors receive their letters of college acceptance they often study less and their grades drop. This phenomenon is popularly known as "senioritis!"

C. INTRINSIC MOTIVATION

1. Based upon personal enjoyment of a task or activity.

2. Artists who paint for enjoyment, volunteers who donate time to community projects, and runners who strive to achieve their personal best time are all intrinsically motivated.

D. OVERJUSTIFICATION

1. What happens when people are given extrinsic rewards for behavior that had been intrinsically motivated? Will the extrinsic reward encourage or discourage performance?

2. Research indicates that extrinsic motivation will displace a person's internal motivation. This is called the overjustification effect.

3. The overjustification effect can sometimes be seen when a musician makes the transition from being an amateur to a professional recording artist. The musician who once played for the joy of making music now performs solely to please producers and make money. As the motivation changed from intrinsic to extrinsic, the performer shows decreased interest and views making music as a job.

III. THE NEUROSCIENCE OF EMOTION

A. THE BRAIN

1. The limbic system comprises a group of brain structures involved in emotion, memory, and basic motivational drives such as hunger, thirst, and sex.

2. The amygdala is part of the limbic system. Several studies have shown that the amygdala plays a key role in emotional responses, especially fear.

B. THE AUTONOMIC NERVOUS SYSTEM

1. The sympathetic nervous system
   ▸ *A subdivision of the autonomic nervous system that arouses body responses.*
   ▸ *When you are emotionally aroused, the sympathetic nervous system causes blood pressure to surge and breathing and heart rates to accelerate. A perceived threat will trigger a fight-or-flight response that includes a dry mouth, dilating pupils, and heavy perspiration.*

2. The parasympathetic nervous system
   ▸ *A subdivision of the autonomic nervous system that calms body responses.*
   ▸ *The parasympathetic nervous system works to calm the body and return it to a more relaxed state.*
   ▸ *The parasympathetic nervous system restores homeostasis immediately after a fight-or-flight response.*

It is very easy to confuse the functions of the sympathetic nervous system and the parasympathetic system. You might link the word "placid," which begins with the letter "P" and means "calm," to the Parasympathetic nervous system, which also begins with the letter "P" and functions to calm the body.

C. POLYGRAPH TESTING

1. The polygraph measures such sympathetic and parasympathetic nervous system responses as heart rate, breathing rate, and galvanic skin response.

2. Autonomic responses change under stress. Contrary to popular belief, the polygraph does not literally measure lying. Instead, it records arousal patterns associated with anxiety and fear. The inference that a person failing a polygraph test has told a lie is based upon the assumption that lying produces arousal of the sympathetic nervous system.

3. It is very important to note that lying is only loosely related to anxiety and fear. Some people remain calm when lying while others become nervous when telling the truth while being questioned in a stressful situation. As a result, polygraph tests cannot infallibly distinguish between innocent and guilty people.

EMOTIONAL EXPRESSION

A. FACIAL EXPRESSION AND EMOTIONS

1. Psychologist Paul Ekman (b. 1934) has conducted the most extensive research on the facial expression of basic emotions.

2. Ekman believes that the "facial language" for basic emotions is innate and thus universal. It is important to note that children who are born deaf and blind nonetheless exhibit facial expressions identical to those of other children.

3. Ekman and his fellow researchers argue that humans exhibit six basic emotions: happiness, sadness, fear, anger, surprise, and disgust. Each emotion is expressed by specific facial expressions. For example, a smile signals happiness on the faces of people across the world.

B. DISPLAY RULES

1. Although facial expressions for basic emotions are universal, cultural display rules influence how and when emotional responses are displayed.

2. In a classic experiment, Ekman showed American and Japanese students films depicting grisly images of surgical procedures. When they watched the film alone, the students all grimaced with disgust at the gruesome scenes. When an official-looking scientist was present, the American students continued to show expressions of disgust. In contrast, the Japanese students masked their negative facial expressions of disgust with a smile. Ekman explained this finding by noting that the Japanese students were following an important display rule. In Japanese culture it is not appropriate to display negative emotions that offend an authority figure.

V. THEORIES OF EMOTION

A. INTRODUCTION—A CONTINUING DEBATE

1. Psychologists agree that emotions include physiological, cognitive, and behavioral components.
2. Psychologists, however, disagree on *how* we become emotional and *which* component of emotion received the most emphasis.

B. THE JAMES-LANGE THEORY OF EMOTION

1. Named after William James (1842–1910) and Carl Lange (1834–1900), the James-Lange theory argues that emotions follow a three-part sequence:
   ▸ *First, you perceive a stimulus. For example, you see a shadowy figure in your backyard.*
   ▸ *Second, the stimulus triggers physiological arousal. When you see the shadowy figure, your heart rate jumps and you begin to tremble.*
   ▸ *Third, you interpret the bodily changes as a specific emotion. In this example, you interpret your pounding heart and trembling as being afraid.*
2. In the James-Lange theory, arousal immediately precedes emotion. James succinctly expressed this sequence when he wrote: "We feel sorry because we cry, angry because we strike, afraid because we tremble."

C. THE SCHACHTER-SINGER TWO-FACTOR THEORY OF EMOTION

1. Psychologists Stanley Schachter (1922–1997) and Jerome Singer agreed with James's view that physiological arousal is a key element in emotion.

2. However, Schachter and Singer point out that physiological arousal is similar for different emotions. In their two-factor theory, Schachter and Singer propose that our emotions depend on physical arousal and the cognitive labeling of that arousal. It is important to know that cognitive labeling is not part of the James-Lange theory.

3. The Schachter-Singer two-factor theory identifies the following sequence of steps:

   ▸ *First, you perceive a stimulus. For example, you see a shadowy figure in your backyard.*

   ▸ *Second, the stimulus triggers both physiological arousal and a cognitive label that makes the best sense of the arousal. In this example, your heart rate jumps and you begin to tremble. You make cognitive sense of the shadowy figure by thinking, "I feel afraid."*

4. In the Schachter-Singer two-factor theory, emotion is the result of the interaction of physiological arousal and the cognitive label we use to explain our condition.

The Schachter-Singer two-factor theory can be applied to a wide variety of everyday experiences. For example, think about how you would feel when you first introduce yourself to the members of a new school club. The members of the club are the stimulus. Your heart rate increases as you introduce yourself. You simultaneously make cognitive sense of this physiological response by thinking, "I'm anxious about meeting new people."

UNDERSTANDING STRESS

A. KEY DEFINITIONS

1. Stress is an emotional response to demands that are perceived as threatening or exceeding a person's resources or ability to cope.
2. A stressor is a trigger that prompts a stressful reaction.

B. CONFLICT AND STRESS

1. Conflict occurs when a person is forced to choose between two or more opposing goals or desires.
2. Approach-approach conflict
   ▸ *Occurs when you are forced to choose between two or more desirable alternatives that both lead to positive results.*
   ▸ *For example, you receive letters of acceptance from your top two colleges. Both colleges have academic and social advantages that make them equally attractive. Which college will you choose to attend? While stressful, an approach-approach conflict ultimately leads to a choice between two desirable options.*
3. Avoidance-avoidance conflict
   ▸ *Occurs when you are forced to choose between two undesirable alternatives that will both lead to negative results.*
   ▸ *For example, you are rejected by all of the colleges to which you applied. You must now choose between getting a job or joining the military. Both options will delay your career goals. Which option will you choose? Avoidance-avoidance conflicts are very stressful because both options are perceived as being undesirable.*
4. Approach-avoidance conflict
   ▸ *Occurs when you are forced to choose an alternative that will have both desirable and undesirable results.*
   ▸ *For example, you receive a letter of acceptance from your top college. You want to attend this college, but it is very expensive. Will you choose this college or one that is less expensive? Approach-avoidance conflicts are*

very stressful because we experience both good and bad
results regardless of what we decide to do.

C. HANS SELYE'S GENERAL ADAPTATION SYNDROME

1. Hans Selye (1907–1982) was a physiologist renowned for his study of stress. Selye identified three progressive stages of stress that collectively form what he called a general adaptation syndrome.

2. The alarm stage
   - *You confront a stress-producing event.*
   - *Your body responds to the stressor by mobilizing internal physical resources. For example, during the alarm stage your body produces adrenaline to bring about the fight-or-flight response.*

3. The resistance stage
   - *Although the intense arousal of the alarm stage diminishes, physiological arousal remains higher than normal.*
   - *Resources are gradually depleted since the body cannot indefinitely maintain a heightened state of arousal.*
   - *This stage can lead to diseases of adaptation, including ulcers and high blood pressure.*

4. The exhaustion stage
   - *Prolonged exposure to the stressor depletes the body's resources.*
   - *Exhaustion leads to physical disorders, vulnerability to illness, collapse, and even death.*

Developmental Psychology

I. STUDYING DEVELOPMENT

A. NATURE VERSUS NURTURE

1. Developmental psychology is the study of age-related changes in behavior and mental processes from conception to death.

2. Led by John Locke (1632–1704), early philosophers argued that at birth our minds were a *tabula rasa* or blank slate. Proponents of the nurturist position continue to argue that development occurs through learning and personal experience.

3. Proponents of the modern nature position emphasize the role of maturation, a sequence of genetically programmed processes of growth and development that occur over time. They also point to the importance of critical periods in maturation. A critical period is a specific time of great sensitivity to age-related learning that shapes the capacity for future cognitive developments.

B. CONTINUITY VERSUS DISCONTINUITY

1. Psychologists who take the continuity approach argue that development is a continuous process as new abilities, skills, and knowledge are added at a gradual pace.

2. In contrast, many psychologists argue that development occurs through a series of distinct stages. Stage theorists devote particular attention to critical periods.

3. Stage theories have played an influential role in developmental psychology. This chapter will devote particular

attention to Jean Piaget's theory of cognitive development, Erik Erikson's psychosocial theory of personality development, and Lawrence Kohlberg's theory of moral development.

C. RESEARCH METHODS

1. The longitudinal method
   - ▸ *The longitudinal method measures a single individual or group of individuals over an extended period of time.*
   - ▸ *The longitudinal method provides in-depth information about age changes. However, it is expensive, time consuming, and typically uses small samples.*
2. The cross-sectional method
   - ▸ *The cross-sectional method compares individuals of various ages at one point in time.*
   - ▸ *The cross-sectional method measures age differences in a large sample of subjects. However, results can be influenced by the fact that the different age groups (known as cohorts) grew up in distinctive historical periods. As a result, it can be difficult to separate age effects from cohort effects.*

II. PRENATAL DEVELOPMENT

A. THE PRENATAL PERIOD

1. The prenatal period begins with conception and ends nine months later with birth.
2. During the first ten days after conception, the fertilized egg or zygote becomes an embryo.
3. During the embryonic stage, cells begin to divide and differentiate into organ systems. After 8 weeks, the developing embryo becomes a fetus.
4. The fetal stage lasts until birth. During this time, neural cells are produced at the astounding rate of 250,000 per minute.

B. TERATOGENS

1. Teratogens are toxic substances that can harm the fetus if ingested or contracted by the mother.

2. Teratogens include drugs, alcohol, nicotine, and viruses, such as HIV and AIDS.
3. Fetal alcohol syndrome is a combination of birth defects, including organ deformities and mental, motor, and/or growth retardation, that result from maternal alcohol abuse.

III. THE NEONATAL OR NEWBORN STAGE

A. SENSORY ABILITIES

1. The neonatal period extends from birth to one month of age.
2. Newborns can respond to sweet, salty, and bitter tastes. They can see close objects, such as their mother's face, but have poor distance vision. Newborns are attracted to female voices and begin to recognize their mother's voice.

B. REFLEXES

1. Newborns are equipped with a variety of behavioral reflexes that help them survive.
2. For example, the grasping reflex enables newborns to cling to their mother (or father); the postural reflex enables newborns to sit with support; and the rooting reflex enables newborns to turn toward the source of a touch and open their mouths.

IV. DEVELOPMENT DURING INFANCY

A. BRAIN DEVELOPMENT

1. Infancy is characterized by rapid growth and development of the brain and nervous system.
2. By the age of 2, an infant's brain is about 75 percent of its adult weight and size.
3. People typically cannot remember events that occurred when they were infants because many brain circuits were not fully connected at the time.

KEY CONTENT REVIEW

B. MOTOR DEVELOPMENT

1. The development of motor skills provides a particularly good illustration of the maturation process.

2. In the typical development of motor skills, infants roll over at 3 months, sit alone at 5.5 months, stand alone at 11.5 months, walk alone at 12 months, and walk up steps at 17 months.

C. LANGUAGE DEVELOPMENT

1. As discussed in Chapter 9, Noam Chomsky and other linguists believe that every child has the innate ability to learn language.

2. Parents in every culture use a distinctive style of speech called motherese or "baby talk" to encourage language development. Motherese uses the distinct pronunciation of simplified words such as "bye-bye" and "night-night."

3. Infants in every culture follow a patterned sequence of language development that begins with "cooing." Infants then begin to babble sounds in their native language at around 9 months of age. Somewhere near their first birthday, infants delight their parents by saying "mama," "dada," and other meaningful words.

4. After producing their first words, infants soon begin the process of combining them into two-word sentences such as "doggie here" and "dada go." Linguistic skills continue to develop rapidly. By the age of three, the typical child has a vocabulary of 3,000 words.

D. MARY AINSWORTH AND ATTACHMENT

1. Attachment is the strong bond of affection that forms between a child and a parent or other regular caregiver.

2. Developmental psychologists distinguish between secure and insecure attachments. A secure attachment forms when parents or caregivers consistently meet the infant's needs by being warm and responsive. In contrast, an insecure attachment forms when parents or caregivers fail to fully meet the infant's needs by being neglectful and inconsistent.

3. Developmental psychologist Mary Ainsworth devised a research procedure called the Strange Situation to measure attachment. In this procedure, Ainsworth placed an infant and his or her mother in an unfamiliar room filled with a variety of toys. A few minutes later, a strange person entered the room and, after a short time, the mother departed. The mother returned a few minutes later and then repeated the pattern of leaving and returning.

4. Ainsworth observed this sequence of repeated separations and reunions through a one-way window. Securely attached infants responded to the Strange Situation by using their mother as a "secure base" to explore the room. They displayed a positive reaction to their mother. In contrast, insecurely attached infants were less likely to explore the room and more likely to display negative reactions to their mother.

5. Current research indicates that the quality of attachment during infancy has a variety of long-term effects. Securely attached infants tend to be well adjusted, form successful social relationships, and perform better at school. Insecurely attached infants tend to form shallow relationships, appear withdrawn, and sometimes display an insatiable need for affection.

E. HARRY HARLOW AND CONTACT COMFORT

1. During the 1940s and 1950s, developmental psychologists believed that infants became attached to those who provided them with nourishment. This widely-held theory ignored the role of physical contact.

2. In a famous series of experiments, Harry Harlow gave orphaned baby monkeys two artificial surrogate "mothers." A cloth "mother" provided no milk but offered a soft terry-cloth cover. A wire "mother" provided milk, but offered no contact comfort.

3. Experimental results documented by particularly poignant pictures showed that in frightening situations the infant monkey clung to the cloth mother even when the wire mother had a nursing bottle.

4. Harlow concluded that the stimulation and reassurance derived from the physical touch of a parent or caregiver play a key role in developing healthy physical growth and normal socialization.

Harlow's famous experiments are vivid and easy to remember. In contrast, Mary Ainsworth's Strange Situation experiments are easy to skim over or ignore. Don't make this mistake. Ainsworth's attachment research was featured in a 2008 free-response question and in recent multiple-choice questions. Be sure you can explain Ainsworth's research procedure as well as the differences between secure and insecure attachments.

V. PIAGET'S THEORY OF COGNITIVE DEVELOPMENT

A. IMPORTANCE

1. Jean Piaget (1896–1980) was a Swiss psychologist whose theories of cognitive development have had a profound impact upon our understanding of how the mind develops. One noted developmental psychologist underscored Piaget's importance when he declared, "Assessing the impact of Piaget on developmental psychology is like assessing the impact of Shakespeare on English literature . . ."

2. Prior to Piaget's research, many assumed that a child's mind was simply a small-scale replica of an adult's mind. Piaget's life-long observations convinced him that children are not less intelligent than adults. They simply think differently.

3. Piaget's stage theory describes how infants, children, and adolescents use distinctively different cognitive abilities to understand the world. Piaget identified four distinct stages of cognitive development. Each stage marks a fundamental change in how a child thinks and understands the world.

B. KEY CONCEPTS

1. Schema
    ▸ *A schema is a concept or framework that organizes and interprets information.*
    ▸ *For example, young children develop a schema for Santa Claus that includes a jolly old man with a white beard who wears distinctive red clothes. Santa rewards good children with gifts and presents on Christmas.*

2. Assimilation
    ▸ *In Piaget's theory, assimilation is the process of absorbing new information into an existing schema.*
    ▸ *For example, as they become older, children see Santa on television and in the mall. Children assimilate these Santas into their existing schema by identifying them as "Santa's helpers."*

3. Accommodation
    ▸ *In Piaget's theory, accommodation is the process of adjusting old schemas or developing new ones to incorporate new information.*
    ▸ *For example, when children become older, they realize that Santa Claus doesn't really exist. Children are forced to develop a new schema that identifies Santa as a fictional character (played by their parents) who nonetheless continues to bring them presents on Christmas.*

C. THE SENSORIMOTOR STAGE

1. The sensorimotor stage begins at birth and lasts until "significant" language acquisition begins at about age 2. During this stage, infants use their senses and motor activities to explore their environment and develop new schemas.

2. At the beginning of this stage, infants lack object permanence—the understanding that objects and people continue to exist even when they cannot be seen, heard, or touched. For example, if a ball rolls under a bed, it is literally out of the infant's sight and thus out of the infant's mind.

3. During their second year, children develop the ability to form internal images or mental representations of objects. Popularly called the "mind's eye," this new ability enables the child to develop object permanence.

D. THE PREOPERATIONAL STAGE

1. In Piaget's theory, the preoperational stage usually lasts from age 2 to age 7. It is important to understand that Piaget uses the word "operations" to refer to logical mental activities. So the "preoperational" stage is really another way of saying the pre-logical stage.

2. Symbolic thought
   ‣ *As children expand their vocabulary they begin to develop the ability to engage in symbolic thought. Symbolic thought refers to the ability to use words, images, and symbols to represent the world.*
   ‣ *For example, a preschool child uses a toy steering wheel to pretend she is driving a car. This type of make-believe play illustrates how children use symbolic thought to imitate their parents.*

3. Egocentrism
   ‣ *Preoperational children often display egocentric thinking. In Piaget's theory, egocentrism does not mean being selfish or conceited. Instead, egocentrism is the inability to consider another person's point of view.*
   ‣ *Because of egocentrism, preoperational children assume that others see, hear, and think exactly as they do. For example, a young girl genuinely believes that a set of Zhu Zhu Pets, complete with a hamster funhouse, would make an ideal birthday present for her grandfather. After all, that is exactly what she wants for her birthday.*

4. Animistic thinking
   ‣ *Children in the preoperational stage believe that inanimate objects, such as the sun, flowers, and clouds, have feelings.*
   ‣ *For example, a preschool child demonstrates animistic thinking when he says, "The sun is happy today," or "The flowers are sad because they need water."*

5. Irreversibility
    ▸ *Irreversibility is the child's inability to mentally reverse a sequence of events or logical operations.*
    ▸ *For example, Jack and Olivia are each given identical cookies. Olivia breaks her cookie into a number of pieces and boasts, "Now I have more to eat than you!" Preoperational Jack is jealous because he cannot mentally reverse the process and think, "If Olivia puts her pieces back together, her cookie would be the same as mine."*

6. Centration
    ▸ *Why can't Jack understand that Olivia's divided cookie is the same as his whole cookie? According to Piaget's theory, preoperational Jack can only focus, or center, on just one aspect of a situation. Because of centration, Jack ignores the equal volume of the cookies, and instead focuses on the number of pieces.*

E. THE CONCRETE OPERATIONAL STAGE

1. The concrete operational stage lasts from roughly age 7 to age 11. During this stage, children can apply logical thought to concrete objects and events.

2. Conservation
    ▸ *In the preoperational stage, children cannot reverse mental steps. However, in the concrete operational stage, children can grasp the concept of reversibility.*
    ▸ *Concrete operational children understand the principle of conservation. In Piaget's theory, conservation is the understanding that two equal quantities remain equal even though their form or appearance is rearranged. Concrete operational Jack would now understand that the broken pieces of Olivia's cookie are, in fact, equal to his whole cookie.*

F. THE FORMAL OPERATIONAL STAGE

1. The formal operational stage is the fourth and final stage of Piaget's theory of cognitive development. It begins in adolescence and continues through adulthood.

2. The capacity to think logically about abstract concepts and hypothetical situations is the hallmark of formal operational thinking.

3. For example, an 8-year-old will explain the concept of dishonesty in concrete personal terms by saying, "Dishonesty is when I don't tell daddy the truth." In contrast, the formal operational adolescent can explain dishonesty by using abstract concepts such as dishonor, disgrace, and integrity.

Although Piaget's theory of cognitive development is a landmark in developmental psychology, it has only played a minor role in free-response questions. AP Psychology test writers prefer to use multiple-choice questions to test such basic Piagetian concepts as accommodation, assimilation, and object permanence. Don't spend valuable study time trying to memorize the definitions of these concepts. Instead, concentrate on being able to recognize illustrative examples of the concepts and stages in Piaget's theory.

G. CRITICISMS OF PIAGET'S THEORY

1. Although contemporary developmental psychologists accept Piaget's basic premise that infants, children, and adolescents have different cognitive abilities, they have challenged and refined aspects of his theory.

2. Researcher Renée Baillargeon used visual tasks to demonstrate that infants as young as 2½ months of age are capable of displaying object permanence.

3. Russian psychologist Lev Vygotsky (1896–1934) placed greater emphasis upon the role of social and cultural factors in influencing cognitive development. For example, a researcher tested the formal operational skills of a Liberian farmer with this logical question: "All Kpelle men are rice farmers. Mr. Smith is not a rice farmer. Is he a Kpelle man?" The Kpelle farmer responded by saying, "I don't know the man. I have not laid eyes on the man myself." The Kpelle farmer relied upon his cultural training instead of formal operational rules of logic. This supports Vygotsky's view that cognitive development takes place within a social and cultural context.

SOCIAL AND EMOTIONAL DEVELOPMENT

A. TEMPERAMENT

1. Temperament is an individual's characteristic manner of behavior. Researchers believe that temperament has a strong genetic base.

2. Jerome Kagan (b. 1929) has identified a number of temperamental patterns. For example, "bold" babies are less easily frightened and more socially responsive than "shy" babies.

3. It is important to note that parenting styles and social interaction can modify a child's temperament. In addition, no one temperament is ideally suited for all social situations. Kagan cautioned his readers to "remember that, in a complex society like ours, each temperamental type can find its adaptive niche."

B. PARENTING STYLES

1. Diana Baumrind (b. 1927) identified three distinct parenting styles.

2. Permissive
   - *Permissive parents set few rules, make minimal demands, and allow their children to reach their own decisions.*
   - *For example, Connor is a 17-year-old senior in high school. His parents left on a weekend trip and left instructions to "take care of the house while we're gone." When Connor's parents returned, they discovered that he had hosted a party and left the house a mess. Connor's parents responded by saying, "You could have made a better decision. We were young once too. We understand that these things happen. Let's clean up the mess and move on."*
   - *Children of permissive parents tend to be impulsive, immature, and often fail to respect others.*

3. Authoritative
   - *Authoritative parents set firm rules, make reasonable demands, and listen to their child's viewpoint, while still insisting on responsible behavior.*

▸ *For example, Lily is a 17-year-old senior in high school. Before leaving on a weekend trip, her parents discussed the "house rules" that Lily would follow. Lily would be permitted to entertain a few of her girlfriends until midnight. When Lily's parents returned, they were shocked to discover that Lily's friends had brought their friends, and a quiet evening quickly turned into a late night party. Lily's parents listened to her explanation, but concluded by insisting "you must be held accountable for breaking the house rules." Lily's parents then grounded her for two weeks and moved up her curfew to 11:00 p.m. until further notice.*

▸ *Children of authoritative parents tend to be well-adjusted, goal oriented, and socially competent.*

4. Authoritarian

▸ *Authoritarian parents set rigid rules, enforce strict punishments, and rarely listen to their child's viewpoint.*

▸ *For example, Landon is a 17-year-old high school senior. Before leaving on a weekend trip, his parents sternly listed a series of fixed rules. They concluded by warning, "Just do it our way, or else!" The rules included a strict prohibition against parties, or even visits by friends. When Landon's parents returned, they learned from a neighbor that he had invited several friends over for a loud party. Landon's furious parents yelled at him and forbade any "backtalk." They then grounded Landon for three months and confiscated his video games.*

▸ *Children of authoritarian parents tend to be moody, aggressive, and often lack good communication skills.*

VII. ERIK ERIKSON'S THEORY OF PSYCHOSOCIAL DEVELOPMENT

A. INTRODUCTION

1. Like Piaget, Erik Erikson (1902–1994) created an influential theory of development.

2. According to Erikson, as we progress from infancy to old age, we enter eight psychosocial stages of development. Each stage corresponds to a physical change. Furthermore, each

stage occurs in a distinctive social setting. This combination of physiological change within a new social environment creates a psychosocial crisis that can be resolved with either a positive or negative response.

3. As maturing individuals work out solutions to these crises, they gradually develop a stable identity. An identity is a person's definition or description of himself or herself.

B. STAGE 1, TRUST VERSUS MISTRUST (BIRTH TO AGE 1)

1. Prior to birth, an infant's physiological needs are automatically taken care of within its mother's womb. After birth, infants are dependent upon adult care for their survival.

2. Erikson emphasized the crucial role played by the mother within the family social setting. Inconsistent, inadequate, and rejecting care can result in a basic mistrust. Consistent, warm, and accepting care will result in what Erikson calls an "inner certainty" or sense of trust that the world is predictable and reliable.

3. For example, an orphaned child who is transferred from foster home to foster home would develop feelings of mistrust, and might avoid becoming emotionally involved with others.

4. It is important to note that if we learn to mistrust adults in our infancy, we may change when we enter school and meet teachers whose behavior encourages trust. Or, if we develop a sense of trust during infancy, we may later become mistrustful if, for example, our parents undergo a bitter divorce.

C. STAGE 2, AUTONOMY VERSUS DOUBT (AGES 1–3)

1. During the second and third years of life, children develop new physical and mental skills. They can walk, climb, grasp objects, push and pull, and, of course, talk. Children are proud of these accomplishments and insist on doing everything themselves.

2. The crisis that now arises stems from a child's growing desire for autonomy. Parents who accept their child's need to control his or her body, impulses, and immediate environment foster a sense of autonomy, preparing the child for independence later in life.

3. However, if parents insist on being overly controlling or harshly critical, they foster a growing sense of doubt and lack of confidence.

D. STAGE 3, INITIATIVE VERSUS GUILT (AGES 3–6)

1. Between the ages of three and six, a child's physical capacities develop to the point where he or she can initiate play activities rather than merely following other children. Young children often engage in play-acting, imagining themselves in a variety of adult roles. They also begin to ask many questions, a sign of intellectual initiative.

2. If parents respect and encourage these efforts, they will enhance their child's sense of initiative. If, however, children are made to feel that their activities are "bad," their play-acting absurd, and their questions a nuisance, they will develop a sense of guilt about self-initiated activities that will be detrimental in later life.

E. STAGE 4, INDUSTRY VERSUS INFERIORITY (AGES 6–12)

1. Between the ages of six and twelve, the social setting expands from the family to school, where children are, for the first time, exposed to formal and impersonal rules.

2. During this time, young children demonstrate industry as they build model planes, construct tree houses, furnish doll houses, and complete school projects.

3. A child's sense of industry will be reinforced if parents and teachers praise his or her creative projects. However, if parents scold a child for "making a mess" and teachers assign a child low grades, they can instill a lasting sense of inferiority.

F. STAGE 5, IDENTITY VERSUS ROLE CONFUSION (ADOLESCENCE)

1. During the teenage years, adolescents mature physically as they enter puberty. At the same time, adolescents become capable of abstract thought. The teenage peer group now provides an important social setting.

2. According to Erikson, this stage of life produces a psychosocial crisis that he calls "identity versus role

confusion." No longer young children, but not yet adults, adolescents struggle to interpret their past, present, and future and combine them into a meaningful sense of identity.

3. Erikson emphasizes the role which culture plays in influencing an adolescent's selection of identity. Role confusion can result from failure to resolve life's earlier crises or from major cultural conflicts, such as war, economic instability, and domestic turmoil.

G. STAGE 6, INTIMACY VERSUS ISOLATION (EARLY ADULTHOOD)

1. According to Erikson, young adults search for a partner to care about and share their lives with. A happy, newly-married couple illustrates the goal of intimacy.

2. Young adults who feel threatened by an intimate relationship will avoid intimacy with another person rather than risk being "swallowed up." A person who is unable to maintain a meaningful relationship with others can become lonely and isolated.

H. STAGE 7, GENERATIVITY VERSUS SELF-ABSORPTION (MIDDLE ADULTHOOD)

1. In this stage, the individual enters middle age. Family and work become the dominant social settings.

2. Erikson defined generativity as "the concern in establishing and guiding the next generation." If this fails, an individual can stagnate and become absorbed with material possessions and personal problems.

I. STAGE 8, INTEGRITY VERSUS DESPAIR (LATE ADULTHOOD)

1. During the last stage of life, a person must come to terms with dying. As a result, Erikson sees this stage as a time of reflection and evaluation.

2. People who can look back and feel that their lives were successful will feel a sense of self-acceptance that Erikson calls integrity.

3. However, people who see their lives as a series of missed opportunities and "might have beens" will probably give in to despair.

VIII. LAWRENCE KOHLBERG'S THEORY OF MORAL DEVELOPMENT

A. INTRODUCTION

1. As we have seen, infants are born with an array of behavioral reflexes. However, an infant is not born with a concept of morality. Moral reasoning or ideas of right and wrong must be learned.

2. Lawrence Kohlberg (1927–1987) was an American psychologist who specialized in research on moral reasoning. His influential theory of stages of moral development is a milestone in developmental psychology.

B. RESEARCH METHODOLOGY

1. Hypothetical moral dilemmas
   ▸ *Kohlberg first created a series of 10 hypothetical moral dilemmas.*
   ▸ *For example, here is the well-known "Heinz Dilemma." In Europe, a woman was near death from a special kind of cancer. There was one drug that doctors thought might save her. It was a form of radium that a druggist in the same town had recently discovered. The drug was expensive to make, but the druggist was charging 10 times what the drug cost him to make. He paid $200 for the radium and charged $2,000 for a small dose of the drug. The sick woman's husband, Heinz, went to everyone he knew to borrow the money, but he could only raise about $1,000, half of what the drug cost. He told the druggist that his wife was dying and asked him to sell it to him cheaper or let him pay later. But the druggist said, "No. I discovered the drug and I'm going to make money from it." Heinz got so desperate, he broke into the druggist's store to steal the drug for his wife. Should the husband have done this?*

2. Interviews
   ▸ *In his original study, Kohlberg presented his moral dilemmas to 72 boys from Chicago-area suburbs. The boys were 10, 13, and 16 years old.*

> ▸ Kohlberg and his associates then interviewed each boy. During the 45-minute recorded interviews, Kohlberg asked participants a series of open-ended questions about the dilemmas. Note that Kohlberg focused on the form of moral reasoning used by each participant.
> ▸ Kohlberg concluded that his participants' responses could be categorized into three levels of moral development.

C. PRECONVENTIONAL MORALITY

1. The preconventional level of moral reasoning is typical of young children. This age group makes moral judgments based upon avoiding punishment. Their egocentric moral reasoning is limited to how their choice will affect themselves.
2. For example, preconventional children typically responded that Heinz should not have stolen the medicine because he would be put in prison and branded a bad person.

D. CONVENTIONAL MORALITY

1. The conventional level of moral reasoning is typical of adolescents and young adults. People at this level make moral judgments based on compliance with society's rules and values. These conventional standards of what is right and wrong are learned from parents, teachers, peers, and media.
2. For example, conventional respondents typically explained that Heinz should not have taken the medicine because stealing would mean breaking the law.

E. POSTCONVENTIONAL MORALITY

1. The postconventional level of moral reasoning is typically expressed by adults. People at this level develop personal standards of right and wrong. They define morality in terms of abstract principles of justice.
2. For example, postconventional respondents argued that Heniz should have stolen the medicine because his wife's right to life superseded the druggist's right to private property.

F. CAROL GILLIGAN'S CRITICISM OF KOHLBERG'S THEORY

1. Researcher Carol Gilligan (b. 1936) criticized Kohlberg for failing to include women in his research design.

2. Gilligan's criticism is based upon her argument that Kohlberg's theory fails to sufficiently account for differences in experience and outlook between males and females. Gilligan contends that the moral concerns of men emphasize justice, while the moral concerns of women focus on caring and compassion.

Kohlberg's theory of moral reasoning can be complex. Do not spend valuable study time trying to memorize each part of his theory. AP Psychology test writers do not ask questions that require you to reproduce or outline detailed stage theories. Instead, know that children progress from a morality based on punishment and reward to one ultimately defined by abstract ethical principles. Also, do not neglect Carol Gilligan's criticism of Kohlberg's theory. Test writers have actually asked as many multiple-choice questions about Gilligan's criticism as about Kohlberg's theory.

Personality

I. SIGMUND FREUD AND THE PSYCHOANALYTICAL PERSPECTIVE

A. INTRODUCTION

1. Personality is an individual's unique and relatively stable pattern of thinking, feeling, and behaving.
2. Sigmund Freud (1856–1939) is the best-known figure in the history of psychology, and one of the seminal figures in twentieth century thought.
3. Freud's psychoanalytic perspective on personality emphasizes the following three factors:
   ▸ *The influence of unconscious mental processes*
   ▸ *The importance of sexual and aggressive instincts*
   ▸ *The enduring consequences of early childhood experiences*

B. LEVELS OF AWARENESS

1. Conscious
   ▸ *According to Freud, the conscious level consists of thoughts or motives that a person is currently aware of or is remembering.*
   ▸ *At this moment, your conscious mind is focusing on studying Freud's psychoanalytic theory of personality as part of your review for the upcoming AP Psychology exam.*
2. Preconscious
   ▸ *According to Freud, the preconscious level consists of thoughts, motives, and memories that can be voluntarily brought to mind.*

▶ *At this moment, your preconscious mind may include feelings of fatigue and hunger, plus random thoughts about what could be on the AP Psychology exam.*

3. Unconscious

▶ *According to Freud, the unconscious level consists of thoughts, feelings, motives, and memories blocked from conscious awareness. Freud believed that the unconscious is not directly accessible. However, dream analysis can be a useful tool for gaining insight into unconscious motives.*

▶ *At this moment your unconscious contains an array of aggressive impulses, sexual desires, and occasional irrational thoughts about not taking the AP Psychology exam.*

C. PERSONALITY STRUCTURE

1. Freud believed that personality is composed of three distinct psychological processes—the id, the ego, and the superego. It is important to remember that these are personality structures and not separate parts of the brain.

2. The id

▶ *According to Freud, the id (Latin for "it") is completely unconscious. It consists of innate sexual and aggressive instincts and drives. The id is impulsive, irrational, and immature. It operates on a pleasure principle, seeking to achieve immediate gratification and avoid discomfort.*

▶ *For example, Ethan's grandmother gave him a large amount of money as a high school graduation present. Rather than using the money to pay for his college tuition, Ethan's id wants to buy a new car.*

3. The superego

▶ *According to Freud, the superego is partly conscious. It consists of internalized parental and societal standards. Popularly known as the "conscience," the superego operates on a morality principle, seeking to enforce ethical conduct.*

▶ *For example, Ethan's superego would oppose using his grandmother's gift to buy a sports car. It would put pressure on Ethan by making him feel guilt, shame, and self-doubt.*

4. The ego
   ▸ *According to Freud, the ego (Latin for "I") resides in the conscious and preconscious levels of awareness. The ego is rational and practical. It operates on a reality principle, seeking to mediate between the demands of the id and the superego. Keenly aware of external realities, the ego attempts to facilitate an appropriate and timely gratification of desires.*
   ▸ *For example, Ethan's ego would mediate a compromise between the aggressive demands of the id that he buy a new sports car and the moral demands of his superego that he use his grandmother's gift for college tuition. Ethan's ego resolves this dilemma by deciding to use most of the money for college tuition while setting aside some money for a less-expensive, used sports car.*

D. EGO DEFENSE MECHANISMS

1. Mediating the conflicting demands of the id and superego is difficult. Anxiety often results when the ego cannot find a realistic compromise. According to Freud, the ego uses unconscious distortions of reality called defense mechanisms to reduce anxiety.

2. Repression
   ▸ *Preventing anxiety-producing thoughts and painful feelings from entering consciousness. Freud believed that repression is the first and most basic form of anxiety reduction.*
   ▸ *For example, you forget the details of what you said when you broke up with your boyfriend or girlfriend.*

3. Projection
   ▸ *Transferring one's own unacceptable thoughts, motives, or personal qualities to others.*
   ▸ *For example, you feel dislike for a coach, and then insist that she dislikes you.*

4. Denial
   ▸ *Protecting oneself from anxiety-producing information by refusing to acknowledge it.*

▸ For example, you refuse to admit that you have a drinking problem although you drink alcoholic beverages every day.

5. Reaction formation

▸ Thinking or behaving in a way that is the opposite of your own unacceptable thoughts and feelings.

▸ For example, you take care of a sick relative whom you actually despise.

6. Displacement

▸ Redirecting anger and other unacceptable impulses toward a less-threatening person or object.

▸ For example, you yell at a teammate after being criticized by your coach.

7. Rationalization

▸ Justifying one's actions by using socially acceptable explanations.

▸ For example, you deal with the disappointment of being rejected by a top college by saying that you really didn't want to attend such an elitist institution.

8. Regression

▸ Retreating from a threatening situation by reverting to a pattern of behavior characteristic of an earlier stage of development.

▸ For example, you throw a temper tantrum when your parents refuse to extend your curfew.

Test Tip

Defense mechanisms have generated a significant number of multiple-choice questions. Test writers favor a format in which the question names a defense mechanism and then asks you to select an example that best exemplifies it.

E. CRITICISMS OF FREUD AND THE PSYCHOANALYTIC PERSPECTIVE

1. Freud's sweeping generalizations are based upon evidence drawn from a small number of patients.

2. Freud's key concepts are impossible to empirically measure.

3. Freud's theories often reflect a sexist view of women.

II. THE NEO-FREUDIANS

A. INTRODUCTION

1. Freud's pioneering theories attracted a number of followers.
2. Alfred Adler (1870–1937) and Carl Jung (1875–1961) are called neo-Freudians because they continued to work within the psychoanalytical perspective while proposing new theories of their own.

B. ALFRED ADLER

1. Adler believed that infants and young children are helpless and dependent upon others. This situation produces deep feelings of weakness, inadequacy, and incompetence that Adler called an inferiority complex.
2. Adler believed that individuals deal with feelings of inferiority in either of two ways:
    ▸ *They can compensate for real or imagined weaknesses by striving to improve themselves and by developing their talents and abilities.*
    ▸ *They can overcompensate for their feelings of inferiority by developing a superiority complex in which they exaggerate their accomplishments and deny their limitations.*

C. CARL JUNG

1. Like Freud, Jung stressed the importance of unconscious processes. However, Jung distinguished between the personal unconscious and the collective unconscious.
2. According to Jung, the personal unconscious consists of experiences that are unique to each individual. In contrast, the collective unconscious refers to that part of a person's unconscious that is common to all human beings.
3. The collective unconscious includes shared human experiences embodied in myths and cultural archetypes such as the wise grandfather, the innocent child, and the rebellious son.

III. THE HUMANIST PERSPECTIVE ON PERSONALITY

A. CARL ROGERS

1. Carl Rogers (1902–1987) rejected Freud's pessimistic view of human nature. Instead, Rogers offered the optimistic view that people are innately good, and thus, "positive, forward-moving, constructive, realistic, and trustworthy."

2. Rogers argued that self-concept is the cornerstone of a person's personality. Self-concept is the set of perceptions and beliefs that individuals have about their own nature and behavior.

3. People whose self-concept matches their life experiences usually have high self-esteem and better mental health.

4. Rogers believed that people are motivated to achieve their full potential or self-actualize. Parents can help their children self-actualize by creating an atmosphere of unconditional positive regard in which a child is accepted and loved without any conditions.

B. ABRAHAM MASLOW

1. Abraham Maslow (1908–1970) shared Rogers' confidence in human nature. He also stressed that humans have a natural drive to find self-fulfillment and realize their potential.

2. Maslow's famous hierarchy of needs is discussed in Chapter 9. It is important to note that Maslow viewed self-actualization as an ongoing process of growth.

 IV. THE SOCIAL-COGNITIVE APPROACH TO PERSONALITY

A. ALBERT BANDURA AND SELF-EFFICACY

1. As you learned in Chapter 8, Albert Bandura (b. 1925) is best known for his "Bobo doll" experiments and his contributions to social learning theory.

2. Bandura is also known for his pioneering work on the concept of self-efficacy. According to Bandura, self-efficacy refers to the feelings of self-confidence or self-doubt that people bring to a specific situation.

3. Self-efficacy varies from situation to situation. For example, a student could have a high degree of self-efficacy in a computer lab, and a low degree of self-efficacy in a dance studio. It is interesting to note that self-efficacy and achievement motivation are highly correlated with success in college.

B. JULIAN ROTTER AND THE LOCUS OF CONTROL

1. Julian Rotter (b. 1916) argued that a person's sense of personal power or locus of control is key in shaping both personality and the manner of approaching a problem.

2. Rotter made an important distinction between internal and external locus of control. Individuals who accept personal responsibility for their life experiences have an internal locus of control. For example, you are displaying an internal locus of control by studying this book as part of your preparation for the AP Psychology exam. In contrast, individuals who believe that most situations are governed by chance and lucky breaks have an external locus of control. An AP Psychology student who refuses to review, and instead counts on catching a lucky break with easy free-response questions, is displaying an external locus of control.

Test Tip

Cognitive psychologists are especially interested in assessing a person's locus of control. Be sure that you can explain and illustrate the difference between an internal locus of control and an external locus of control. For example, a person with an internal locus of control would carefully prepare for a job interview, while a person with an external locus of control would count on luck.

V. **TRAIT THEORIES**

A. EARLY TRAIT THEORIES

1. A trait is a relatively stable personal characteristic that can be used to describe how an individual consistently behaves.

2. Gordon Allport (1897–1967) used a comprehensive dictionary to develop a list of 4,504 adjectives that could be used to describe specific personality traits. He then arranged these traits into the following three levels:

   ▶ *Cardinal traits that dominate and shape a person's outlook*
   ▶ *Central traits that influence most of our behavior*
   ▶ *Secondary traits that are only seen in certain situations*

3. Needless to say, the traits on Allport's list proved to be confusing and overlapping. Raymond Cattell (1905–1998) used a statistical technique, called factor analysis, to reduce Allport's list to 171 terms. He later refined this list to 16 key personality factors. This led to the development of a personality measure known as the Sixteen Personality Factor Questionnaire or 16PF.

B. DEVELOPMENT OF THE FIVE-FACTOR MODEL OF PERSONALITY

1. Led by Paul Costa and Robert McCrae, personality theorists continued to refine the list of traits as they searched for the basic underlying dimensions of personality.

2. Costa and McCrae's research ultimately led to the development of the Five-Factor Model, popularly called the "Big Five Model."

C. THE BIG FIVE

1. Openness

   ▶ *People with high scores on openness tend to be intellectually curious, open to experience, interested in cultural pursuits, and sensitive to beauty.*
   ▶ *People with low scores on openness tend to be conventional thinkers who prefer straightforward answers and regard the arts and sciences with suspicion.*

> ▸ *Examples of openness statements include, "I have a vivid imagination," "I spend time reflecting on things," and "I have a rich vocabulary."*

2. Conscientiousness

> ▸ *People with high scores on conscientiousness tend to be self-disciplined, well-organized, and motivated to achieve personal goals.*
>
> ▸ *People with low scores on conscientiousness tend to be careless, impulsive, and undependable.*
>
> ▸ *Sample conscientiousness items include, "I am always prepared," "I follow a schedule," and "I pay attention to details."*

3. Extroversion

> ▸ *People with high scores on extroversion tend to be sociable, talkative, and enthusiastic. They like to draw attention to themselves in groups.*
>
> ▸ *People with low scores on extroversion tend to be reserved, quiet, and prefer time alone.*
>
> ▸ *Examples of extroversion statements include, "I am the life of the party," "I start conversations," and "I feel comfortable around people."*

4. Agreeableness

> ▸ *People with high scores on agreeableness tend to be trusting, cooperative, and helpful.*
>
> ▸ *People with low scores on agreeableness tend to be suspicious, argumentative, and uncooperative.*
>
> ▸ *Examples of agreeableness statements include, "I make people feel at ease," I take time out for others," and "I am interested in other people's problems."*

5. Neuroticism

> ▸ *People with high scores on neuroticism tend to be insecure, easily upset, anxious, and moody.*
>
> ▸ *People with low scores on neuroticism tend to be calm, easygoing, and emotionally stable.*
>
> ▸ *Examples of neuroticism statements include, "I get irritated easily," I worry about things," and "I am relaxed most of the time."*

D. CRITICISMS OF THE BIG FIVE MODEL

1. The Big Five Model underestimates the variability of behavior from situation to situation. For example, a person could

be very extroverted in a setting where he or she feels comfortable and very reserved in a setting where he or she feels uncomfortable.

2. The Big Five Model does a good job of describing personality. However, it does not do a good job of explaining why people develop personality traits.

3. The Big Five Model neglects such key personality dimensions as religiosity, manipulativeness, and sense of humor.

A generation of psychologists used factor analysis to winnow Allport's original list of 4,504 adjectives in the Five Factor Model. Remembering the five factors is easy. The first letter of each dimension—openness, conscientiousness, extroversion, agreeableness, and neuroticism—spells the word OCEAN!

VI. PERSONALITY ASSESSMENT

A. PROJECTIVE TESTS

1. Projective tests are derived from psychoanalytic approaches to personality. They use ambiguous images, such as inkblots and pictures of people, that are open to a number of interpretations. The subject's response is thought to be a projection of his or her unconscious conflicts, motives, and personality traits into the test images.

2. The Rorschach Inkblot Test

   ▸ *Swiss psychiatrist Hermann Rorschach (1884–1922) developed the first projective test in 1921. Although Rorschach died the following year, his pioneering work led to the inkblot test that now bears his name.*

   ▸ *The Rorschach test consists of 10 cards with symmetrical inkblot images. The examiner carefully records the subject's responses, paying close attention to descriptions of animate and inanimate objects and human and animal figures.*

3. The Thematic Apperception Test (TAT)

  ▸ *The Thematic Apperception Test (TAT) uses a series of provocative, but ambiguous, pictures. Subjects are asked to tell a dramatic story that includes what led up to the event, what is happening at the moment depicted, what the characters are feeling, and what the outcome of the story is.*

  ▸ *Like the Rorschach test, the TAT is intended to reveal the subject's unconscious motivation and personality characteristics.*

4. Evaluating projective tests

  ▸ *Proponents argue that projective tests produce a wealth of information that can yield important insights into an individual's personality.*

  ▸ *Critics argue that projective tests are time-consuming, expensive, and subjective.*

B. SELF-REPORT INVENTORIES

1. Self-report tests contain inventories of multiple-choice and true-false questions designed to differentiate people on a particular personality characteristic.

2. The Minnesota Multiphasic Personality Inventory (MMPI)

  ▸ *The MMPI contains over 500 statements. Subjects respond to each statement by answering "True," "False," or "Cannot say." Sample questions include, "I am often very tense on the job," and "I wish I could do over some of the things I have done."*

  ▸ *Clinical psychologists and psychiatrists use the MMPI to diagnose psychological disorders. It is important to note that the MMPI is not a vocational interest test.*

3. Evaluating self-report inventories

  ▸ *Proponents argue that self-report inventories are standardized, objective, and relatively inexpensive to administer and score.*

  ▸ *Critics argue that respondents can give false answers to hide their true feelings. In addition, many people are not good judges of their own behavior.*

Testing and Individual Differences

I. THEORIES OF INTELLIGENCE

A. WHAT IS INTELLIGENCE?

1. Psychologists have vigorously debated the nature of intelligence. For example, is intelligence a single general ability? Or is intelligence a cluster of different mental abilities?

2. Psychologist David Wechsler (1896–1981) formulated the following widely-accepted definition of intelligence: "The global capacity to think rationally, act purposefully, and deal effectively with the environment."

B. CHARLES SPEARMAN AND THE G FACTOR

1. During the 1920s, British psychologist Charles Spearman (1863–1945) observed that an individual's scores on various tests of intellectual performance correlated with one another. That is, people who performed well on a test of one mental ability, such as mathematical reasoning, tended to also do well on verbal ability and other tests.

2. Based upon this observation, Spearman proposed that intelligence is a single underlying factor, which he termed general intelligence or the g factor.

3. Spearman concluded that the g factor could be expressed as a single number, such as an IQ score.

C. RAYMOND CATTELL AND THE TWO SUBTYPES OF G

1. Raymond Cattell's research studies led him to conclude that Spearman's concept of general intelligence could be broken

down into two relatively independent components that he called fluid and crystallized intelligence.

2. Fluid intelligence (gf)
    ▸ *Fluid intelligence includes memory, speed of information processing, and reasoning abilities, such as forming new concepts, seeing underlying relationships, and quickly solving unfamiliar problems.*
    ▸ *Cattell believed that fluid intelligence is innate and thus independent of education and experience.*
    ▸ *Note that fluid intelligence, like other biological capacities, declines with age.*

3. Crystallized intelligence (gc)
    ▸ *Crystallized intelligence refers to the store of knowledge and skills gained through experience and education.*
    ▸ *Crystallized intelligence remains stable or increases slightly with age.*

Make sure you know the difference between fluid intelligence and crystallized intelligence. Remember that "fluid" means to flow and fluid intelligence changes throughout life. In contrast, "crystallize" means to take a definite form. Crystallized intelligence takes a definite form and remains stable, or even increases slightly, as a person ages.

D. ROBERT STERNBERG AND THE TRIARCHIC THEORY OF INTELLIGENCE

1. Contemporary cognitive theorists now believe that intelligence is a collection of separate and different abilities.

2. Robert Sternberg's (b. 1949) triarchic theory of intelligence identifies the following three aspects of intelligence:
    ▸ *Analytical intelligence—logical reasoning skills that include analysis, evaluation, and comparison.*
    ▸ *Creative intelligence—imaginative skills that include developing new inventions and seeing new relationships.*
    ▸ *Practical intelligence—practical "street smart" skills that include coping with people and events.*

3. Sternberg believes that each of these three intelligences is learned, and therefore, can be developed and enhanced.

E. HOWARD GARDNER AND MULTIPLE INTELLIGENCES

1. Howard Gardner (b. 1943) points out that different cultures recognize and value different abilities. For example, the Hapsburg rulers of Austria prized and rewarded musical skills. As a result, musical geniuses, such as Mozart and Beethoven, transformed Vienna into the music capital of Europe.

2. Gardner believes that musical intelligence is one of a number of "multiple intelligences" that are recognized and defined within the context of each culture. Gardner's ever-growing list of intelligences ranges from the linguistic skills demonstrated by writers to the kinesthetic skills demonstrated by athletes.

II. THE DEVELOPMENT OF INTELLIGENCE TESTS

A. ALFRED BINET

1. During the early 1900s, French psychologist Alfred Binet (1857–1911) designed a series of tests to measure the mental abilities of school children. Binet focused on mental abilities such as memory and the ability to distinguish similarities and differences.

2. Binet soon discovered that brighter children performed like older children. For example, a bright 8-year-old might be able to answer the same number of questions as an average 10-year-old. This insight led Binet to make a distinction between a child's mental age and a child's chronological age.

3. Binet used his new test to compute an average score for each age level. He then compared each child's performance against the average abilities of a given age group. For example, if a child's score was the same as the average score for a group of 8-year-olds, the child was said to have the mental age (MA) of an 8-year-old, regardless his or her chronological age (CA).

KEY CONTENT REVIEW

B. LEWIS TERMAN AND THE STANFORD-BINET INTELLIGENCE TEST

1. Binet's pioneering work impressed Stanford University psychologist Lewis Terman (1877–1956). Within a short time, Terman developed a revised test that he called the *Stanford-Binet Intelligence Scale.*

2. Terman used the following formula to compute a child's intelligence quotient or IQ:

   IQ = Mental Age (MA) divided by Chronological Age (CA) × 100

3. For example, an 8-year-old child who correctly answered the same number of questions as a 10-year-old would have a mental age of 10. Using the Stanford-Binet IQ formula, the child would have an IQ of 10/8 × 100 or 125.

C. DAVID WECHSLER AND THE WECHSLER INTELLIGENCE SCALES

1. David Wechsler (1896–1981) strongly believed that intelligence involved a variety of mental abilities. First published in 1955, the *Wechsler Adult Intelligence Scale* (WAIS) yielded separate verbal and performance scores.

2. Like the Stanford-Binet test, Wechsler's test yielded a final single IQ score. However, Wechsler used a new approach to calculate the IQ score. Instead of using the Stanford-Binet's IQ formula, Wechsler determined how far a person's score deviates from the scores of others in the same group. The group scores formed a bell-shaped curve with a statistically fixed mean score of 100. This normal distribution means that 34 percent of individual scores are one standard deviation or 15 points below 100 and another 34 percent are one standard deviation or 15 points above 100. Thus, 68 percent of all individuals score between 85 and 100. Today, the Stanford-Binet and most other intelligence tests use this system.

3. In addition to his test for adults, Wechsler developed intelligence tests for preschool and school age children. The Wechsler tests are now the most widely-used measures of intelligence.

PRINCIPLES OF TEST CONSTRUCTION

A. STANDARDIZATION

1. Suppose you correctly answered 40 of 50 questions on an intelligence test. Did you perform well or poorly?

2. In order to determine how well you performed, your score must be compared to a standard of performance. Standardization means that the test has been uniformly presented to a large, representative sample of people. The scores of this representative group set the norms or standards against which the performance of later test takers can be evaluated.

3. Standardized norms for the Stanford-Binet and the Wechsler tests all form a bell-shaped curve so that 68 percent of the scores occur within one standard deviation above or below the mean.

B. RELIABILITY

1. A trustworthy test must be reliable. Reliability means that a test must produce consistent results when it is administered on repeated occasions.

2. Reliability can be determined by the test-retest method in which researchers compare participants' scores on two separate administrations of the same test. The test demonstrates a strong reliability if there is a high positive correlation between the two test scores.

3. Reliability can also be determined by a procedure known as the split-half method. In this procedure, a test is divided into two equivalent parts. The researcher then determines the degree of similarity between scores on the two halves of the test. For example, there should be a very high correlation between the odd and even numbered questions on a test.

C. VALIDITY

1. A trustworthy test must also demonstrate validity. Validity is the ability of a test to measure what it was designed to measure.

2. Criterion validity is a key measure of test validity. Tests demonstrate criterion validity when test scores can be used to predict another relevant measure. For example, your AP Psychology exam is an achievement test designed to measure your knowledge of the material in a college-level introductory psychology course. The AP Psychology exam would demonstrate criterion validity if high scores on it are correlated with high scores in college psychology courses.

The concepts of reliability and validity consistently generate a number of multiple-choice questions. In order to nail down the definition of reliability, you might mentally connect the "R" in reliability with the "R's" in repeatable results. Remember that a test can be reliable without being valid. For example, a driver's education course could have a written test that demonstrates reliability, but is not correlated with how well a student performs on an actual road test.

IV. EXTREMES IN INTELLIGENCE: INTELLECTUAL DISABILITY AND GIFTEDNESS

A. INTELLECTUAL DISABILITY (INTELLECTUAL DEVELOPMENTAL DISORDER)

1. Characterized by deficits in intellectual and adaptive functioning with four levels of severity (mild, moderate, severe, and profound).
2. Genetic abnormalities, such as Down syndrome can cause intellectual disability. Prenatal exposure to alcohol, drugs, or other teratogens can also cause intellectual disability.

B. INTELLECTUAL GIFTEDNESS

1. The label "intellectually gifted" is applied to individuals who score significantly above average in general intellectual functioning.
2. Only about 1 to 3 percent of people are classified as being intellectually gifted.

2. Lewis Terman's study of gifted children

  ▸ *Lewis Terman conducted the best-known and most extensive study of gifted children. Terman identified 1,528 California grade school children with IQs of 140 or higher. He then conducted a longitudinal study by tracking the children's progress through school and into adulthood.*

  ▸ *Affectionately known as the "Termites," the gifted children went on to achieve a high level of academic and career success. Although most of the Termites led happy and fulfilling lives, their high IQ did not guarantee success. For example, the group's divorce rate nearly equaled the national average.*

 V. TEST SCORES AND THE SELF-FULFILLING PROPHECY

A. THE SELF-FULFILLING PROPHECY

1. IQ and other test scores can be very powerful labels that affect how others see a person and how a person sees himself or herself.

2. A self-fulfilling prophecy occurs when a person's expectations of another person leads that person to behave in the expected way.

B. A STUDY

1. Robert Rosenthal and Lenore Jacobson tested the effects of the self-fulfilling prophecy in an unidentified elementary school called "Oak School." The researchers informed elementary school teachers that about 20 percent of their students were academically gifted "spurters." In reality, Rosenthal and Jacobson randomly selected the "spurters."

2. At the end of the year, the teachers demonstrated a self-fulfilling prophecy when they reported that the "spurters" were more curious, happier, and better adjusted than the other students. The "spurters" academic performance proved to be consistent with their teacher's biased expectations. They achieved high grades and made substantial gains in IQ points.

The concept of the self-fulfilling prophecy has played a particularly prominent role in the free-response questions of the AP Psychology exam. For example, in 1995, test writers asked students to explain how the self-fulfilling prophecy contributes to prejudice. In 2000, a free-response question asked how the self-fulfilling prophecy might affect student performance in a school without grades. It is very important to remember that a self-fulfilling prophecy can have both positive and negative effects.

VI. THE IMPACT OF HEREDITY AND ENVIRONMENT ON INTELLIGENCE

A. HEREDITY

1. Studies of identical twins support the hypothesis that intelligence is, in part, inherited. For example, the IQ correlation for pairs of identical twins is greater than for pairs of fraternal twins.

2. Studies of adopted children show that their IQs are more strongly correlated with their biological mother's IQ than with their adoptive mother's IQ.

B. ENVIRONMENT

1. Studies of identical twins reared separately support the hypothesis that environment plays an important role in determining IQ. For example, the correlation between the IQ scores of identical twins reared separately is lower than those of identical twins reared together.

2. Studies also find that early enrichment programs can have a positive impact on children's IQ scores.

Abnormal Behavior

I. IDENTIFYING ABNORMAL BEHAVIOR

A. FOUR BASIC STANDARDS

1. Abnormal behavior is unusual. It occurs infrequently in a given population.
2. Abnormal behavior is maladaptive. It interferes with a person's ability to function normally in one or more important areas of life.
3. Abnormal behavior is disturbing to others. It represents a serious departure from social and cultural norms of behavior.
4. Abnormal behavior is distressful. It prevents a person from thinking clearly and making rational decisions.

B. THE DIAGNOSTIC AND STATISTICAL MANUAL OF MENTAL DISORDERS (DSM-5)

1. DSM-5 stands for the *Diagnostic and Statistical Manual of Mental Disorders*, Fifth Edition.
2. Clinicians and researchers from a wide range of specialized areas collaborated to create the manual. The DSM-5 provides a set of diagnostic categories for classifying over 300 specific psychological disorders.
3. The DSM-5 lists the criteria and specific symptoms for each mental disorder, and is designed to generate reliable and valid diagnoses.

Test Tip

Be sure that you can identify the Diagnostic and Statistical Manual of Mental Disorders (DSM-5) as the handbook used by medical and mental health professionals for the diagnosis of mental illness. The DSM-5 typically generates at least one multiple-choice question on each AP Psychology exam.

II. THEORIES OF ABNORMAL BEHAVIOR

A. THE PSYCHOANALYTIC PERSPECTIVE

1. The psychoanalytic perspective views mental disorders as the product of intrapsychic conflicts among the id, the ego, and the superego.

2. In order to protect itself, the ego represses psychic conflicts into the unconscious. These conflicts result from unresolved traumatic experiences that took place in childhood. For example, rejection can produce strong feelings of anger. The psychoanalytic perspective views depression as anger that is channeled into the unconscious.

B. THE HUMANIST PERSPECTIVE

1. The humanist perspective looks to a person's feelings, self-esteem, and self-concept for the causes of mental behavior.

2. Humanists believe that behavior is the result of choices we make in struggling to find meaning in life. For example, anxiety can result when an individual experiences a gap between his or her ideal self and his or her real self.

C. THE COGNITIVE PERSPECTIVE

1. The cognitive perspective focuses on faulty, illogical, and negative ways of thinking.

2. Maladaptive thoughts lead to misperceptions and misinterpretations of events and social interactions. For example, unrealistically negative thoughts can lead to depression.

D. THE BEHAVIORIAL PERSPECTIVE

1. The behavioral perspective stresses that abnormal behavior is learned.

2. Behaviorists focus on how a behavior was reinforced and rewarded. For example, during classical conditioning, a stimulus that was originally neutral (such as an elevator) becomes paired with a frightening event (the power going out) so that it becomes a conditioned stimulus that elicits anxiety.

E. THE BIOLOGICAL PERSPECTIVE

1. The biological perspective argues that many psychological disorders are caused by hormonal or neurotransmitter imbalances, differences in brain structure, and inherited predispositions.
2. For example, an imbalance of a chemical that influences the nervous or endocrine system can cause anxiety.

 ## III. ANXIETY DISORDERS

A. GENERAL CHARACTERISTICS

1. Anxiety disorders all involve extreme levels of fear and anxiety which negatively impact behavior and cognitive processes. They differ in terms of the types of scenarios which generate fear or anxiety, and in what types of thoughts result.
2. Anxiety is a feeling of tension, apprehension, and worry that occurs during a personal crisis or the pressures of everyday life.
3. Anxiety is a normal human response to stress. In contrast, pathological anxiety is irrational, uncontrollable, and disruptive.
   ▸ *Pathological anxiety is irrational because it is provoked by nonexistent or exaggerated threats.*
   ▸ *Pathological anxiety is uncontrollable because the person cannot control or stop anxiety attacks.*
   ▸ *Pathological anxiety is disruptive because it impairs relationships and everyday activities.*
4. Generalized anxiety disorder, panic disorder, phobias, and agoraphobia are the main types of anxiety disorders.

B. GENERALIZED ANXIETY DISORDER (GAD)

1. Characterized by persistent, uncontrollable, and ongoing apprehension about a wide range of life situations.
2. This free-floating anxiety can lead to chronic fatigue and irritability. GAD affects twice as many women as men.

KEY CONTENT REVIEW

C. PANIC DISORDER

1. Characterized by sudden episodes of extreme anxiety in the form of panic attacks and the persistent concern about having future attacks.
2. Panic attacks are accompanied by a pounding heart, rapid breathing, sudden dizziness, and a feeling of lightheadedness.

D. PHOBIAS

1. Characterized by a strong, irrational fear of specific objects or situations that are normally considered harmless. For example, Howie Mandel, the well-known comedian, actor and television host, has mysophobia, fear of germs. Howie refuses to shake hands with contestants and, instead, exchanges fist bumps.

E. AGORAPHOBIA

1. Characterized by an irrational fear of public places or open spaces due to the concern that the individual will not be able to escape or receive help if needed.
2. Agoraphobics avoid crowded locations such as airports, stores, concerts, or college campuses. In extreme cases they may be unable to leave their own home.

IV. OBSESSIVE-COMPULSIVE AND RELATED DISORDERS

A. GENERAL CHARACTERISTICS

1. Characterized by unwanted anxiety producing thoughts and/or repetitive behaviors.
2. Obsessive-compulsive disorder, body dysmorphic disorder, hoarding, and trichotillomania (hair-pulling disorder) are the main disorders in this category.

B. OBSESSIVE-COMPULSIVE DISORDER

1. Characterized by persistent unwanted thoughts (obsessions), which often cause distress or anxiety and/or repetitive behaviors (compulsions) the individuals feel they must perform in order to reduce anxiety.

2. Obsessions and compulsions are time consuming and cause significant distress. Compulsive behaviors can include excessive washing, repeatedly checking to make sure that doors are locked, and turning lights on and off.

C. HOARDING

1. Characterized by persistent difficulty and distress with regard to giving up possessions, and an excessive need to save items including those with no value.
2. The hoarding behaviors result in significant levels of personal distress or disrupt normal functioning in occupational, family, or social settings.

V. TRAUMA- AND STRESSOR-RELATED DISORDERS

A. GENERAL CHARACTERISTICS

1. Characterized by exposure to a traumatic or stressful event.
2. Posttraumatic stress disorder (PTSD) and acute stress disorder are the main disorders in this category.

B. POSTTRAUMATIC STRESS DISORDER

1. Characterized by the exposure to actual or threatened death, serious injury, or violence resulting in feelings of horror and helplessness. Individuals can also develop PTSD if they learn that a traumatic event happened to a close friend or family member.
2. People who suffer from PTSD experience intrusive symptoms including reoccurring, involuntary, and distressing memories of the event. This disorder can lead to depression, anxiety, uncontrollable crying, edginess, and the inability to concentrate.

VI. DEPRESSIVE DISORDERS

A. GENERAL CHARACTERISTICS

1. Depressive disorders are serious disturbances in a person's emotions that involve loss of pleasure, sleep problems, lack

of concentration, negative thoughts, or a suicidal ideation. Depressive disorders cause psychological discomfort and impair a person's ability to function.

2. Major depression, persistent depressive disorder (dysthymia), and disruptive mood dysregulation disorder are the main types of depressive disorders.

B. MAJOR DEPRESSIVE DISORDER

1. Characterized by a lasting and continuous depressed mood. People suffering from major depression often feel deeply discouraged and lethargic. Pulitzer Prize-winning author William Styron described his depression as being "like some poisonous fogbank rolling in upon my mind, forcing me into bed. There I would lie for as long as six hours, stuporous and virtually paralyzed, gazing at the ceiling . . ."

2. Major depression often leads to suicidal feelings. Approximately 10 percent of those suffering major depression attempt suicide. For example, Kurt Cobain, the lead singer and guitarist of the rock band Nirvana, had a long history of depression. Cobain committed suicide in 1994 when the 27-year-old musician was at the height of his fame.

VII. BIPOLAR AND OTHER RELATED DISORDERS

A. GENERAL CHARACTERISTICS

1. Characterized by periods of both depression and mania or hypomania.
2. Bipolar disorders were formerly considered types of mood disorders, but were made into a separate category in the DSM-5.
3. Bipolar I, bipolar II, and cyclothymic disorder are the main types of bipolar and related disorders.

B. BIPOLAR I DISORDER

1. Characterized by periods of both depression and mania. During a manic episode the individual is hyperactive and may not sleep for days at a time. Sufferers frequently exhibit racing thoughts known as flight of ideas, a shortened attention span, and an inflated sense of importance.

2. The bipolar roller coaster has affected a number of creative writers and artists. For example, Edgar Allan Poe and Vincent van Gogh both showed signs of bipolar disorder.

 VIII. SOMATIC SYMPTOM AND RELATED DISORDERS

A. GENERAL CHARACTERISTICS

1. Characterized by physical complaints or conditions resulting in significant personal distress and impairment.
2. Somatic symptom disorder, conversion disorder, and factitious disorder are the main disorders in this category.

B. SOMATIC SYMPTOM DISORDER

1. Characterized by physical complaints that are either extremely distressing or that prevent normal functioning. Individuals experience persistent symptoms that may or may not have a known medical cause.
2. Individuals often have an exaggerated concern about health and illness. They may frequently meet with physicians and devote excessive amounts of time to researching symptoms and illnesses.

C. CONVERSION DISORDER

1. Characterized by paralysis, blindness, deafness, or other loss of sensory or motor control, with no discernible physical cause despite neurological examination.
2. The symptom or symptoms results in significant distress or impaired functioning.

 IX. SCHIZOPHRENIA

A. PREVALENCE AND IMPORTANCE

1. Schizophrenia affects approximately 1 percent of the U.S. population.
2. Approximately half of all people admitted to mental hospitals are diagnosed with schizophrenia.
3. Schizophrenia typically begins in late adolescence or early adulthood. It rarely emerges prior to adolescence or after age 45.

KEY CONTENT REVIEW

4. Schizophrenia is equally prevalent in men and women.

B. CHARACTERISTIC SYMPTOMS

1. Delusional beliefs
    ▸ *A delusion is a bizarre or farfetched belief that continues in spite of competing contradictory evidence.*
    ▸ *People suffering from schizophrenia often experience delusions of persecution or grandeur. In a delusion of persecution, people believe that spies, aliens, or even neighbors are plotting to harm them. In a delusion of grandeur, people believe they are someone very powerful or important, such as an Old Testament king or a modern ruler.*

2. Hallucinations
    ▸ *A hallucination is a false or distorted perception that seems vividly real to the person experiencing it.*
    ▸ *Although hallucinations can be visual, or even olfactory, people with schizophrenia often report hearing voices that comment on their behavior or tell them what to do.*

3. Disorganized speech and thought
    ▸ *Disorganized speech and thought includes creating artificial words and jumbling words and phrases together. This incoherent form of speech is often called a word salad.*
    ▸ *A lack of contact with reality is the most common thought disturbance experienced by people with schizophrenia.*

4. Emotional and behavioral disturbances
    ▸ *The emotions of people with schizophrenia range from exaggerated and inappropriate reactions to a flat affect, showing no emotional or facial expressions.*
    ▸ *People with schizophrenia often exhibit unusual and wide-ranging behaviors, from shaking the head to remove unwanted thoughts to assuming an immobile stance for an extended period of time.*

C. EXPLAINING SCHIZOPHRENIA

1. The genetic basis for schizophrenia
    ▸ *The lifetime risk of developing schizophrenia increases with genetic similarity. People who share more genes with a person who has schizophrenia are more likely to develop the disorder.*

KEY CONTENT REVIEW

▶ Schizophrenia tends to cluster in certain families.

▶ Adoption studies have consistently shown that if either biological parent has schizophrenia, the adopted individual is at a greater risk to develop schizophrenia.

▶ If one identical twin develops schizophrenia, the risk rate for the other twin is 48 percent.

2. The dopamine hypothesis

▶ According to the dopamine hypothesis, overactivity of certain dopamine neurons in the brain may contribute to some forms of schizophrenia.

▶ Drugs that increase the amount of dopamine can produce or worsen some symptoms of schizophrenia.

▶ Drugs that block dopamine activity can reduce or eliminate some symptoms of schizophrenia.

3. The diathesis-stress model

▶ People may have either an inherited or environmental predisposition that increases their risk for schizophrenia (diathesis).

▶ Stressful life experiences then trigger schizophrenic episodes.

Schizophrenia is by far the most tested type of abnormal behavior on the AP Psychology exam. It always generates at least one, and often two, multiple-choice questions. The 2007 AP Psychology exam devoted an entire free-response question to schizophrenia. Be sure you can identify hallucinations, delusions, and fragmented thinking as key symptoms of schizophrenia. In addition, review the research findings that support the dopamine hypothesis and the genetic basis for schizophrenia.

X. PERSONALITY DISORDERS

A. GENERAL CHARACTERISTICS

1. Well-adjusted people are able to modify their personality traits as they adjust to different social experiences. In contrast, people with personality disorders are inflexible and maladaptive across a broad range of situations.

2. Personality disorders usually become evident during adolescence or early adulthood.

3. Narcissistic personality disorder and antisocial personality disorder are two of the best-known (and most frequently tested) personality disorders.

B. NARCISSISTIC PERSONALITY DISORDER

1. Characterized by a grandiose sense of self-importance, fantasies of unlimited success, need for excessive admiration, and a willingness to exploit others to achieve personal goals.

2. The etiology or causes of narcissistic personality disorder are unknown. Researchers currently believe that excessive admiration that was never balanced with realistic feedback may be an important causal factor.

C. ANTISOCIAL PERSONALITY DISORDER

1. Characterized by a profound disregard for, and violation of, the rights of others. Individuals with antisocial personality disorder lack a conscience and show no remorse for actions that harm others. They often display insight into the weaknesses of others and are surprisingly poised when confronted with their destructive behavior.

2. Serial killers are often seen as the classic example of people with antisocial personality disorder. For example, in the movie *Batman: The Dark Knight*, the Joker robs banks, kills rivals, blows up a hospital, and attempts to destroy a ferry filled with innocent passengers without experiencing any remorse. Note that antisocial personality disorders are not restricted to serial killers. Approximately 6 percent of men and 1 percent of women display characteristics of antisocial personality disorder. Ruthless politicians and mercenary businesspeople can also display the characteristics of antisocial personality disorder.

3. Antisocial personality disorder does not indicate an individual who is shy or overly reserved. Individuals who have excessive levels of social inhibition would be described as having an avoidant personality disorder.

XI. DISSOCIATIVE DISORDERS

A. GENERAL CHARACTERISTICS

1. Dissociative disorders all involve a splitting apart of significant aspects of a person's awareness, memory, or identity.

2. Individuals who experience dissociative disorders have a compelling need to escape from anxiety and stress.

3. Dissociative identity disorder (DID) and dissociative amnesia are the main disorders in this category.

B. DISSOCIATIVE IDENTITY DISORDER (DID)

1. Characterized by the presence of two or more distinct personality systems in the same individual. Each personality has its own name, unique memories, behaviors, and self image.
2. Despite the revisions in the DSM-5 many researchers and mental health professionals continue to question if DID is a genuine psychological disorder. Skeptics believe that many of the reported cases are not supported by strong scientific evidence.

C. DISSOCIATIVE AMNESIA

1. Characterized by a partial or total inability to recall past experiences, autobiographical information, and important information that is different from normal forgetting.
2. Individuals may have amnesia for specific events or an overall amnesia for their personal identity and life history.
3. Typically a response to traumatic events or extremely stressful situations such as marital problems and military combat.
4. May be accompanied by dissociative fugue which is sudden and inexplicable travel associated with amnesia. While in a fugue state the person experiences amnesia, but can otherwise function normally.

XII. THE ROSENHAN STUDY: THE INFLUENCE OF DIAGNOSTIC LABELS

A. THE PSEUDOPATIENT EXPERIMENT

1. In 1973, David Rosenhan and 7 mentally healthy associates presented themselves for admission to 12 psychiatric hospitals in 5 states. The pseudopatients claimed to hear voices that said, "empty," "hollow," and "thud." Other than this, the pseudopatients acted normally and reported no other psychiatric problems.

2. All of the psychiatric hospitals admitted the pseudopatients. Seven were diagnosed with schizophrenia, and one was diagnosed with manic-depressive psychosis.

3. The hospitals kept the pseudopatients for stays ranging from 7 to 52 days, with an average of 19 days. All were released with a diagnosis of schizophrenia "in remission."

4. It is interesting to note that while all of the mental health professionals failed to detect the ruse, many of the patients correctly realized that the pseudopatients were pretending to be mentally ill.

B. "THE STICKINESS OF THE DIAGNOSTIC LABEL"

1. Rosenhan's study demonstrates the power and danger of what he called the "stickiness of the diagnostic label."

2. The label "schizophrenia" quickly became the central characteristic that governed how the staff treated each pseudopatient. For example, when a pseudopatient wrote down notes, the staff perceived this "writing behavior" as another manifestation of the underlying pathology.

C. SIGNIFICANCE

1. Rosenhan's report, "On Being Sane in Insane Places," provoked a storm of controversy and widespread debate about the positive and negative consequences of diagnostic labels.

2. It is important to note that Rosenhan does not deny the existence of psychological disorders. However, his study underscored the point that a diagnostic label can result in subsequent distortions of the meaning of an individual's behavior.

Test Tip

The Rosenhan study shook the mental health profession by raising important questions about the validity and impact of psychiatric labels. Be sure to review the study and be prepared to discuss the positive and negative consequences of diagnostic labels.

Treatment of Abnormal Behavior

I. THREE APPROACHES TO THERAPY

A. INSIGHT THERAPIES

1. Insight therapies are designed to help clients understand the causes of their problems. This understanding or insight will then help clients gain greater control over their thoughts, feelings, and behaviors.
2. The leading insight approaches include psychoanalytic/psychodynamic, cognitive, and humanistic therapies. All three are based upon a personal relationship between the client and therapist. A variety of group therapies based upon insight are also available for families and married couples.

B. BEHAVIOR THERAPY

1. Behavior therapy focuses on the problem behavior itself, rather than on insights into the behavior's underlying causes.
2. Behavior therapy is based on the principles of classical conditioning, operant conditioning, and observational learning.

C. BIOMEDICAL THERAPY

1. Biomedical therapies are based on the premise that the symptoms of many psychological disorders involve biological factors, such as chemical imbalances, disturbed nervous system functions, and abnormal brain chemistry.
2. Biomedical therapy uses drugs and electroconvulsive therapy to treat psychological disorders.

II. SIGMUND FREUD AND PSYCHOANALYSIS

A. INTRODUCTION

1. Freud's theories of psychoanalysis rest upon the premise that unconscious conflicts and repressed memories are the underlying causes of abnormal behavior.

2. During psychoanalysis, the therapist helps the patient gain insight into how childhood conditions created unconscious conflicts.

3. Insight does not occur easily or quickly. According to Freud, the ego utilizes a variety of defense mechanisms to repress unconscious conflicts and thoughts.

B. FIVE MAJOR PSYCHOANALYTIC TECHNIQUES

1. Encouraging free association
   - *In free association, the patient lays on a couch and spontaneously reports thoughts, feelings, and mental images.*
   - *The psychoanalyst asks questions to encourage the flow of associations in order to provide clues as to what the patient's unconscious wants to conceal.*

2. Analyzing dreams
   - *Freud believed that dreams are symbolic representations of unconscious conflicts and repressed impulses.*
   - *Freud analyzed his patient's dreams as a means of interpreting their unconscious conflicts, motives, and desires.*

3. Analyzing resistance
   - *Resistance is the patient's conscious or unconscious attempt to conceal disturbing memories, motives, and experiences.*
   - *Freud believed that the therapist must help a patient confront and overcome resistance.*

4. Analyzing transference
   - *Transference is the process by which a patient projects or transfers unresolved conflicts and feelings onto the therapist.*
   - *Freud believed that transference helps patients gain insight by reliving painful past relationships.*

5. Offering interpretation
   ▸ *The techniques of psychoanalysis create a close relationship between a patient and his or her psychoanalyst.*
   ▸ *The psychoanalyst waits for the right opportunity to offer a carefully timed interpretation of the patient's hidden conflicts.*

C. EVALUATION

1. Psychoanalysis seems to work best for articulate, highly motivated patients who suffer from anxiety disorders.
2. Psychoanalysis is both time-consuming and expensive.

III. COGNITIVE THERAPY

A. INTRODUCTION

1. Cognitive therapy rests on the assumption that faulty thoughts, such as negative self-talk and irrational beliefs, cause psychological problems.
2. While psychoanalysts focus on unconscious conflicts, cognitive therapists help their patients change the way they think about and interpret life events.

B. ALBERT ELLIS

1. Albert Ellis (1913–2007) noted that most people believe that their emotions and behaviors are the direct result of specific events. For example, a poor SAT or ACT score makes you feel miserable and depressed.
2. Ellis challenged this common-sense interpretation by arguing that our feelings are actually produced by the irrational beliefs we use to interpret events. For example, it is not the poor SAT or ACT score that makes you feel miserable, but rather your irrational belief that since you did not achieve a high score, you are a complete failure.

KEY CONTENT REVIEW

C. RATIONAL EMOTIVE THERAPY

1. Ellis developed a four-step rational emotive therapy (RET) to help his clients recognize and change their self-defeating thoughts.

2. Identifying activating events
    ▸ *RET therapy begins by identifying an "activating event" that affects a client's mental processes and behavior.*
    ▸ *For example, you are nervous during a job interview and are not hired.*

3. Identifying belief systems
    ▸ *The second step in RET therapy is to identify the client's irrational beliefs and negative self-talk.*
    ▸ *For example, you interpret the poor job interview by telling yourself, "I can't stay calm during a job interview. I'll never get a job."*

4. Examining emotional consequences
    ▸ *RET therapists argue that irrational beliefs lead to self-defeating behaviors, anxiety disorders, and depression.*
    ▸ *For example, a disappointing job interview leads to a feeling of depression that reinforces irrational beliefs.*

5. Disputing erroneous beliefs
    ▸ *In the final step of RET therapy, the therapist vigorously disputes the client's faulty logic and self-defeating "should," "must," "can't," and "never" beliefs.*
    ▸ *For example, a therapist would challenge the statement, "I will never get a job because I get too nervous during a job interview."*
    ▸ *Changing irrational beliefs is not easy. Replacing negative self-talk with rational beliefs requires time and patience. For example, the therapist would suggest that the client make the following statement instead: "I can stay calm and confident during an interview and I will find the perfect job for me."*

D. AARON BECK'S COGNITIVE THERAPY

1. Aaron Beck (b. 1921) developed a form of cognitive therapy that has proven to be particularly effective for treating depression.

2. Beck helps his clients come to grips with negative beliefs about themselves, their worlds, and their futures.

3. Beck argues that depression-prone people are particularly susceptible to focusing selectively on negative events while ignoring positive events. In addition, depression-prone people typically engage in all-or-nothing thinking by believing that everything is either totally good or totally bad.

E. EVALUATION

1. Cognitive therapy has proven to be a highly effective treatment for anxiety disorders, depression, addiction, anger management, and bulimia nervosa.

2. Cognitive therapy has been criticized for relying too heavily on rationality while ignoring the client's unconscious drives.

> *Albert Ellis and Aaron Beck have both made significant contributions to cognitive therapy. AP Psychology test writers have thus far placed a greater emphasis upon Ellis's rational emotive therapy (RET). Be sure you know that rational emotive therapy can involve a confrontational atmosphere between the therapist and the client.*

IV. HUMANIST THERAPY

A. INTRODUCTION

1. Humanist psychologists do not view human nature as irrational or self-destructive. Instead, humanist psychologists contend that people are innately good and motivated to achieve their highest potential. When people are raised in an accepting atmosphere, they will develop healthy self-concepts and strive to find meaning in life.

2. People with problems must strive to overcome obstacles that disrupt their normal growth potential and impair their self-concepts.

B. CARL ROGERS AND CLIENT-CENTERED THERAPY

1. Carl Rogers (1902–1987) was an influential humanist psychologist who developed the client-centered approach to therapy.

2. Also called person-centered therapy, client-centered therapy is one of the most widely used models in psychotherapy. In this technique, the therapist creates a comfortable, non-judgmental environment by demonstrating empathy and unconditional positive regard toward his or her patients.

3. Unlike psychoanalysts and cognitive therapists, client-centered therapists do not offer a carefully timed interpretation or a vigorous challenge to their client's beliefs. Instead, client-centered therapists create a non-directive environment in which their clients are encouraged to freely find solutions to their problems.

4. The following exchange illustrates the nondirective approach utilized by client-centered therapists:

    Client: I feel totally rejected. I'm too shy and I'll never be popular.

    Therapist: I guess you feel that way a lot, don't you? That people dismiss you. It's hard to have feelings like that.

    Note that a client-centered therapist does not challenge the client's beliefs. Instead, the therapist actively listened and then paraphrased and clarified what the client said.

C. EVALUATION

1. Humanistic therapy emphasizes the positive and constructive role each individual can play in controlling and determining their mental health. As a result, humanistic psychology has helped remove some of the stigma attached to therapy.

2. Client-centered therapy is unstructured and very subjective. As a result, it is difficult to objectively measure such basic humanistic concepts as self-actualization and self-awareness.

V. GROUP, FAMILY, AND MARITAL THERAPIES

A. INTRODUCTION

1. The psychoanalytic, cognitive, and humanist approaches all focus on the problems of a single client.
2. In contrast, group, family, and marital therapists work with small groups of clients.

B. GROUP THERAPY

1. In group therapy, a number of people meet and work toward therapeutic goals.
2. Although group therapists can and do draw upon a variety of therapeutic approaches, they often base their sessions on the principles of humanistic therapy developed by Carl Rogers.
3. Self-help groups offer a popular variation on group therapy. For example, Alcoholics Anonymous is one of the best-known self-help groups.

C. FAMILY AND MARITAL THERAPIES

1. Family and marital therapists strive to identify and change maladaptive family interactions.
2. Note that families are highly interdependent. When one member has a problem, it affects all the others.

D. EVALUATION

1. Group, family, and marital therapies are less expensive than traditional one-on-one therapies. In addition, group members can gain valuable insights by sharing experiences with others who face similar problems.
2. Group, family, and marital therapies have successfully dealt with alcoholism, drug problems, teenage delinquency, and marital infidelity.

VI. BEHAVIOR THERAPIES

A. INTRODUCTION

1. Although valuable, insight into a problem does not always guarantee desirable changes in behavior and emotions. For example, a student who is extremely anxious about taking the SAT or ACT may understand that he or she feels that way because of a lack of self-confidence caused by demanding parents. However, this insight may do little to reduce the student's high level of test anxiety.

2. Behavior therapists seek to modify specific problem behaviors. Instead of searching for underlying causes rooted in past experiences, behavior therapists focus on the problem behavior itself.

3. Behavior therapists assume that both adaptive and maladaptive behaviors are learned. They therefore attempt to use the principles of classical conditioning, operant conditioning, and observational learning to modify the problem behavior.

B. MARY COVER JONES AND THE BEGINNING OF BEHAVIOR THERAPY

1. Mary Cover Jones (1896–1987) conducted pioneering research in applying behavioral techniques to therapy. As a result, Jones is often called "the mother of behavior therapy."

2. In her first and most famous study, Jones treated a three-year-old named Peter, who was especially afraid of a tame rabbit. Jones used a technique now known as counterconditioning to modify Peter's behavior by associating his favorite snack of milk and crackers with the rabbit. As Jones slowly inched the rabbit closer to Peter in the presence of his favorite food, the little boy grew more comfortable and was soon able to touch the rabbit without fear.

C. JOSEPH WOLPE AND SYSTEMATIC DESENSITIZATION

1. Mary Cover Jones's pioneering work influenced the South African psychologist Joseph Wolpe. During the 1950s, Wolpe perfected a technique for treating anxiety-producing phobias that he named systematic desensitization.

2. Systematic desensitization uses the principles of classical conditioning to reduce anxiety.

3. Systematic desensitization is a behavior therapy in which phobic responses are reduced by first exposing a client to a very low level of the anxiety-producing stimulus. Once no anxiety is present, the client is gradually exposed to stronger and stronger versions of the anxiety-producing stimulus. This continues until the client no longer feels any anxiety toward the stimulus.

4. The three-step desensitization process—

   ▸ *Wolpe begins by teaching his client how to maintain a state of deep relaxation. Recall that the sympathetic nerves are dominant when we are anxious, and the opposing parasympathetic nerves function when we are relaxed. As a result, it is physiologically impossible to be both relaxed and anxious at the same time.*

   ▸ *Wolpe and his client next create a hierarchy or ranked listing of anxiety-arousing images and situations. The list begins with situations that produce minimal anxiety and escalate to those that arouse extreme anxiety.*

   ▸ *Wolpe and his client begin the process of desensitization with the least threatening experience on the anxiety hierarchy. For example, a student who is anxious about taking the SAT or ACT might begin by sitting in the empty classroom where the test will be administered. To extinguish the test anxiety, the student then gradually works his or her way to the top of the hierarchy of anxiety-producing experiences.*

Systematic desensitization has generated a significant number of multiple-choice questions. It is very important to remember that systematic desensitization relies upon classical conditioning to treat specific phobias.

D. AVERSION THERAPY

1. In contrast to systematic desensitization and its use of classical conditioning to reduce anxiety, aversion therapy uses the principles of classical conditioning to create anxiety.

KEY CONTENT REVIEW

2. In aversion therapy, the therapist deliberately pairs an aversive or unpleasant stimulus with a maladaptive behavior. For example, a nausea-producing drug called Antabuse is often paired with alcohol to create an aversion to drinking.

E. EVALUATION

1. Behavior therapy has proven to be an effective way to treat phobias, eating disorders, and obsessive-compulsive disorders.
2. Critics point out that the newly acquired behaviors may disappear if they are not consistently reinforced. Critics also question the ethics of using rewards and punishments to control a client's behavior.

VII. BIOMEDICAL THERAPIES

A. INTRODUCTION

1. Biomedical therapies use drugs and electroconvulsive therapy to treat psychological disorders.
2. In most cases, a psychiatrist must prescribe biomedical therapies.

B. PSYCHOPHARMACOLOGY

1. Psychopharmacology is the study of how drugs affect mental processes and behavior.
2. Antianxiety drugs
   ▸ *Designed to reduce anxiety and produce relaxation by lowering sympathetic activity of the brain.*
   ▸ *Valium and Xanax are the best-known antianxiety drugs.*
3. Antipsychotic drugs
   ▸ *Designed to diminish or eliminate hallucinations, delusions, and other symptoms of schizophrenia. Also known as neuroleptics or major tranquilizers.*
   ▸ *Antipsychotic drugs work by decreasing activity at the dopamine synapses in the brain.*

> ▸ Long-term use of antipsychotic drugs can produce a movement disorder called tardive dyskinesia. The symptoms of tardive dyskinesia include involuntary movements of the tongue, facial muscles, and limbs.

4. Mood-stabilizing drugs
   > ▸ Designed to treat the combination of manic episodes and depression characteristic of bipolar disorders.
   > ▸ Lithium is the best-known drug for treating bipolar disorders.

5. Antidepressant drugs
   > ▸ Designed to treat depression by inhibiting the reuptake of the neurotransmitter serotonin.
   > ▸ Prozac is the best-known and most widely used selective serotonin reuptake inhibitor (SSRI).

KEY CONTENT REVIEW

Test Tip

AP Psychology textbooks often contain detailed charts listing psychological disorders and the drugs used to treat them. Do not waste valuable study time memorizing these lists. You should focus on remembering that Lithium is used to treat bipolar disorders and Prozac is a selective serotonin reuptake inhibitor (SSRI) used to treat depression.

C. ELECTROCONVULSIVE THERAPY

1. In electroconvulsive therapy (ECT), two electrodes are placed on the outside of the patient's head and a moderate electrical current is passed through the brain.

2. Electroconvulsive therapy is used to treat serious cases of depression. Because it works faster than antidepressant drugs, electroconvulsive therapy is often used to treat suicidal patients.

D. EVALUATION

1. Biomedical therapies can be very effective treatments for bipolar disorders and depression. The availability of new drugs has enabled mental hospitals to implement a policy of deinstitutionalizing or releasing patients.

2. Although biomedical drugs relieve many symptoms, they do not cure the underlying disorder and can have many negative side effects. In addition, some patients can become physically dependent on the drugs.

Social Psychology

I. ATTRIBUTIONAL THEORY

A. THE FUNDAMENTAL ATTRIBUTION ERROR

1. Definition
   ▸ *The widespread tendency to overemphasize dispositional factors and to underestimate situational factors when making attributions about the cause of another person's behavior.*
   ▸ *Dispositional factors include personality traits, such as level of motivation and willingness to work.*
   ▸ *Situational factors refer to social influences, such as the absence of parents or group pressures to conform.*

2. Causes
   ▸ *The just-world phenomenon—Most people have a need to believe that the world is just and fair. As a result, they believe that people generally get what they deserve. The just-world phenomenon helps explain the tendency of people to blame the victim rather than to look at social causes.*
   ▸ *The saliency bias—Situational factors are less salient or noticeable than dispositional factors. As a result, people focus on visible personality traits rather than the less visible social context.*

3. Examples
   ▸ *In 2005, Hurricane Katrina devastated the Gulf Coast claiming almost 2,000 lives in New Orleans alone. Why did so many residents of New Orleans fail to evacuate the city? Many critics ignored situational factors, such as the shortage of public transportation, and instead*

focused on dispositional factors, such as residents who foolishly ignored warnings to evacuate the city.
- As you are driving down the road, another car suddenly passes you and speeds through a red light. Most people make the fundamental attribution error by attributing the driver's reckless behavior to dispositional factors, such as drunk driving or aggressive behavior. Few people pause to consider that situational factors may be at work. For example, the driver may be ill and rushing to a nearby hospital.

B. THE SELF-SERVING BIAS

1. Definition
   - Most people take credit for their successes while at the same time attributing their failures to external situations beyond their control.
2. Causes
   - Most people are motivated by a need for self-esteem and a desire to save face.
   - Individuals are more aware of the situational factors that influence their behavior.
3. Examples
   - Students who earn high scores on the SAT and ACT attribute their success to dispositional factors, such as hard work and extensive practice. Students who earn low SAT and ACT scores blame situational factors such as inept teachers, poor test-taking conditions, and tricky questions.
   - Stockbrokers who produce high returns for their clients attribute their success to dispositional factors, such as exhaustive research and disciplined investing. Stockbrokers who produce low returns for their clients blame situational factors, such as unpredictable actions by foreign governments and surprise decisions by the Federal Reserve Board.

C. CULTURAL AND ATTRIBUTIONAL BIASES

1. Individualistic cultures
   - Individualistic cultures, like the United States and Canada, emphasize independence and personal responsibility.

> ▸ *People in individualistic cultures are more likely to commit both the fundamental attribution error and the self-serving bias.*

2. Collectivistic cultures
> ▸ *Collectivistic cultures, like Japan and China, emphasize inter-dependence and collective responsibility.*
> ▸ *People in collectivistic cultures are less likely to make the fundamental attribution error and more likely to be aware of how situational factors influence behavior.*

The fundamental attribution error and the self-serving bias have generated more multiple-choice questions than any other social psychological concepts. Questions typically ask you to apply these concepts to a situation from everyday life. For example, when students attribute their high history grades to hours of extra study and their low chemistry grades to impossible test questions, they are exhibiting the self-serving bias.

II. ATTITUDE FORMATION AND CHANGE

A. DEFINITION

1. An attitude is a positive, neutral, or negative evaluation of a person, issue, or object.
2. Attitudes predispose our reactions to people, issues, or objects.

B. ATTITUDE CHANGE

1. Central route to persuasion
> ▸ *When people focus on factual information, logical arguments, and a thoughtful analysis of pertinent details.*
> ▸ *For example, a car buyer bases his or her decision on such factual factors as a car's gas mileage, its rating by outside experts, the quality of air bags, antilock brakes, seat belts and other safety features.*

2. Peripheral route to persuasion
   ▸ *When people focus on emotional appeals and incidental cues.*
   ▸ *For example, a car buyer bases his or her decision on such incidental factors as the likeability of the car dealer, the car's color, and catchy sales slogans.*

3. Foot-in-the-door phenomenon
   ▸ *The persuasion strategy of getting a person to agree to a modest first request as a set-up for a later, much larger, request.*
   ▸ *For example, a car dealer persuades you to buy a car with upgraded seats and then convinces you to buy the car with a complete upgraded interior. Another common example of the foot-in-the-door phenomenon occurs when volunteers ask you to sign a petition and then follow-up with a request for a donation to their cause.*

C. ATTITUDE CHANGE: COGNITIVE DISSONANCE

1. Definition
   ▸ *The theory of cognitive dissonance was first proposed by Leon Festinger, a research psychologist at Stanford.*
   ▸ *Cognitive dissonance is the state of psychological tension, anxiety, and discomfort that occurs when an individual's attitude and behavior are inconsistent.*
   ▸ *Festinger explained that, "if a person is induced to do or say something that is contrary to his private opinion, there will be a tendency for him to change his opinion to bring it into correspondence with what he has said or done."*
   ▸ *Festinger believed that human beings are motivated to reduce the tensions resulting from inconsistent attitudes and actions. Although it is possible to reduce dissonance by changing either one's behavior or one's attitude, most people modify their attitudes.*

2. Examples
   ▸ *Kristin is aware that smoking is harmful to her health. According to cognitive dissonance theory, Kristin will most likely resolve the tension between her attitude and her behavior by denying the relationship between*

smoking and lung cancer or rationalizing that smoking is a social activity that helps her fit in with her friends.

▸ *Austin impulsively buys an expensive pair of sneakers that he really cannot afford. He then rationalizes the purchase by insisting that the shoes were a good buy and they will improve his basketball performance.*

III. THE INFLUENCE OF GROUPS ON INDIVIDUAL BEHAVIOR

A. SOCIAL FACILITATION AND SOCIAL INHIBITION

1. Social facilitation is the tendency for an individual's performance to improve when simple or well-rehearsed tasks are performed in the presence of others.

2. Social inhibition is the tendency for an individual's performance to decline when complex or poorly-learned tasks are performed in the presence of others.

3. Examples

   ▸ *James Michaels and his associates (1982) found that the performance of expert pool players improved when they played in front of an audience. In contrast, poor players performed worse when they played in front of an audience.*

   ▸ *The presence of an audience often inspires well-trained actors and dancers to raise their performance to a new level. However, the pressure of an audience can have the opposite effect upon poorly prepared actors and dancers.*

B. SOCIAL LOAFING

1. Social loafing is the phenomenon of people making less effort to achieve a goal when they work in a group rather than when they work alone.

2. Causes

   ▸ *People believe that their contribution to the collective effort is neither appreciated nor important.*

   ▸ *People believe they will "get a free ride" since it will be difficult to assess their contribution to the team or group.*

3. Examples
   ▸ *An art teacher divides his class into groups and assigns each group the task of preparing an oral report on a famous Renaissance artist. Each group will select one member to present their report. Since all members of the group will receive the same grade, the method invites social loafing.*
   ▸ *The local animal shelter previously published a report listing the names of individual contributors. However, the new shelter director switched to a report that simply listed the total contribution. The change in reporting made contributors feel less appreciated and important, thus inviting social loafing and a decline in individual contributions.*

C. DEINDIVIDUATION

1. Deindividuation refers to the reduction of self-awareness and personal responsibility that can occur when a person is part of a group whose members feel anonymous.
2. Causes
   ▸ *Individuals become immersed in a group and lose a sense of self-awareness.*
   ▸ *The growing sense of anonymity lowers personal accountability so that individuals no longer feel responsible for their actions. The group thus "assumes" responsibility for aggressive or destructive actions that individuals would not commit if they were alone.*
3. The Stanford Prison Experiment
   ▸ *In August 1971, psychology professor Philip Zimbardo converted the basement of Stanford University's psychology building into a mock prison.*
   ▸ *Zimbardo placed ads in local papers offering to pay volunteers $15.00 a day to participate in a two-week "prison simulation."*
   ▸ *Zimbardo and his team of research assistants selected 24 middle-class, educated young men. The participants were then randomly assigned to the role of either guard or prisoner.*

> ▸ *Zimbardo deliberately promoted the deindividuation of both the guards and the prisoners. The guards wore identical khaki uniforms and mirror sunglasses that prevented anyone from seeing their eyes or reading their emotions. They also carried billy clubs, whistles, and handcuffs. The prisoners all wore stocking caps and hospital dressing gowns. They were identified by numbers sewn into their gowns.*

> ▸ *The experiment quickly grew out of hand as some of the guards turned sadistic, humiliating the prisoners verbally and physically. Alarmed by the guards' cruel behavior, Zimbardo called off the experiment after just six days.*

> ▸ *The Zimbardo Prison Experiment provides a vivid illustration of the powerful effects of deindividuation. As the guards became immersed in their roles, they developed a strong group cohesion that reduced their sense of personal responsibility. As they stopped viewing the prisoners as individual human beings, the guards' behavior became increasingly aggressive.*

D. THE BYSTANDER EFFECT

1. The bystander effect is a social psychological phenomenon in which individuals are less likely to assist in an emergency situation when other people are present.

2. Causes

> ▸ *Group size is the best predictor of bystander intervention. As the size of a group present at the scene increases, the likelihood that anyone will help a person in need decreases.*

> ▸ *As the size of the group increases, bystanders experience a diffusion of responsibility. Since responsibility is not explicitly assigned, bystanders assume that someone else will act. Each individual bystander feels less responsible and thus fails to do anything.*

3. The case of Kitty Genovese

> ▸ *Kitty Genovese was a 28-year-old woman who managed a late-night bar in Queens, New York. At 3:20 a.m. on March 13, 1964, a serial rapist and murderer attacked Ms. Genovese as she approached her apartment building.*

▸ *Although Ms. Genovese repeatedly screamed for help, none of the neighbors came to her aid. After 30 minutes, someone finally called the police. The police rushed to the scene only to find that Ms. Genovese had been fatally wounded.*

4. Conditions that promote bystander intervention

▸ *Kitty Genovese's tragic death focused public attention on the reasons why bystanders failed to come to her rescue. Initially, editorial writers blamed apathy and the depersonalization of life in big cities.*

▸ *Led by Bibb Latane and John Darley, social psychologists conducted hundreds of investigations into the conditions under which bystanders will help others.*

▸ *Researchers found that bystanders are more likely to help if they see others who are willing to help, if they know or are told how to provide assistance, and if the person in trouble asks a specific person to provide assistance.*

IV. GROUP DECISION MAKING

A. GROUP POLARIZATION

1. Definition

▸ *The tendency for a group's predominant opinion to become stronger or more extreme after an issue is discussed.*

▸ *It is important to note the difference between group polarization and conformity. Group polarization is an intensification of a group's prevailing opinion. In contrast, conformity occurs when an individual changes his or her attitude to become more like the group's attitude.*

2. Examples

▸ *Myers and Bishop (1970) discovered that discussing racial issues decreased prejudice in a low-prejudice group of high school students and increased it in a high-prejudice group.*

▸ *Discussions among a stop-smoking self-help group increase the members' resolve to quit smoking.*

B. GROUPTHINK

1. Definition
   ▶ *The tendency for a cohesive decision-making group to ignore or dismiss reasonable alternatives.*
   ▶ *Leaders can counteract groupthink by encouraging divergent views, consulting outside experts, and assigning people to play the role of "devil's advocate."*

2. Examples
   ▶ *In early 1961, President Kennedy and his team of national security advisors approved an ill-conceived plan to allow 1,200 anticommunist exiles to invade Cuba in an attempt to overthrow Fidel Castro. Castro's forces easily repelled the invasion, handing President Kennedy a humiliating defeat.*
   ▶ *In 2003, President Bush and his team of national security advisors approved an invasion of Iraq designed to overthrow Saddam Hussein and locate his presumed arsenal of weapons of mass destruction. The United States successfully defeated Saddam Hussein's forces, but failed to find any weapons of mass destruction.*

V. SOCIAL INFLUENCE: CONFORMITY

A. DEFINITION

1. Conformity is the tendency for people to adopt the behavior, attitudes, and beliefs of other members of a group.
2. Conformity can be in response to real or imagined group pressure.

B. THE ASCH CONFORMITY EXPERIMENTS

1. The Asch conformity experiments are considered the most famous studies of the factors associated with conformity to group pressure.
2. Asch began his experiments by inviting seven to nine male students into a college classroom. One of these students was a "naïve subject" who was unaware of the experiment's true purpose. All the others were "instructed students" who had

previously met with Asch and had carefully rehearsed their experimental roles.

3. By pre-arranged agreement, the instructed students took their seats, always leaving a seat near the end for the naïve subject. By placing his subjects in this order, Asch insured that the naïve subject would receive "the full impact of the majority trend before uttering his judgments."

4. When the subjects were in their seats, Asch showed them a series of cards. A standard line was always clearly displayed on the left. Three companion lines numbered 1, 2, and 3 were always on the right. Asch asked each subject to pick the companion line that matched the standard line.

5. Unknown to the naïve subject, on twelve of the eighteen trials the instructed subjects deliberately gave the wrong answer. Thus, on twelve trials the naïve subject was confronted with a contradiction between what he clearly saw and what a unanimous majority reported.

6. Asch found that 76 percent of the naïve subjects agreed with the incorrect majority opinion at least once, while 5 percent conformed every time. All together, the naïve subjects followed the majority by giving the wrong answer on 37 percent of the critical trials.

C. FACTORS THAT PROMOTE CONFORMITY

1. The size of the majority
   ▸ *Asch varied the size of the informed majority by using groups of between one and fifteen people.*
   ▸ *Asch found that the naïve subjects resisted groups of only one or two members. However, conformity increased as the size of the informed majority increased from three to seven members.*
   ▸ *Interestingly, as group size increased beyond seven members, conformity leveled off and slightly decreased.*

2. The unanimity of the majority
   ▸ *The unanimity of the majority made a striking impact on the amount of conformity.*
   ▸ *When Asch planted a "partner" who disagreed with the majority, conformity by the naïve subjects dropped to about one-fourth of its former level.*

3. The characteristics of the majority
   ▸ *Conforming behavior was greatest among naïve subjects who were attracted to the group.*
   ▸ *Naïve subjects, who expected to have future interaction with the group and had a relatively low status in the group, demonstrated the highest levels of conformity.*
4. The difficulty of the task
   ▸ *As the difficulty of the experimental task increased, conformity increased.*
   ▸ *Asch reported a higher level of conformity when the difference between the standard line and the companion line was smaller.*

 ## VI. SOCIAL INFLUENCE: OBEDIENCE TO AUTHORITY

A. DEFINITION

1. Obedience is the performance of an action in response to the direct orders of an authority or person of higher status.

B. MILGRAM'S OBEDIENCE EXPERIMENTS

1. Milgram's famous experiments on obedience began in July 1961 at Yale University. Milgram's controversial findings sparked debate about the willingness of ordinary citizens to obey an authority figure who instructed them to perform actions that conflicted with their personal values. In addition, Milgram's use of deception influenced the debate about the proper code of ethics in psychological research.
2. Milgram's basic experimental design involved three people:
   ▸ *An experimenter played by a 31-year-old high school biology teacher. The experimenter wore a white technician's coat to enhance his status as an authority figure.*
   ▸ *A learner or victim played by an affable 47-year-old Irish-American accountant.*

> ▸ *A teacher or subject who responded to an ad offering volunteers $4.00 (equal to approximately $30.00 today) to participate in a one-hour "memory and learning test." The subjects represented a wide range of educational and occupational backgrounds.*

3. The experimenter began by explaining that he was testing the effects of punishment on learning and memory. The learner would be required to memorize a long list of word pairs such as "slow-dance," "nice-day," and "blue-box." The learner was later required to pick the correct match from a list of several words read by the volunteer teacher. For example, the teacher would read: "Blue: sky, ink, box, lamp" and the learner was supposed to respond, "box."

4. When the learner gave the correct answer, the teacher would proceed to the next word pair. However, when the learner made a mistake, the experimenter instructed the teacher to punish him with an electric shock delivered by a realistic, but bogus, shock generator.

5. The shock generator could supposedly deliver shocks ranging from 15 volts to 450 volts. The 30 switches were clearly labeled from "Slight Shock" up to "Danger: Severe Shock." The 435-volt and 450-volt switches were simply marked "XXX."

6. The experimenter instructed the teacher to begin with a 15-volt shock and then raise the voltage one 15-volt level at a time. It is important to note that the volunteer teacher was given a 45-volt sample of "Slight Shock." This was the only real shock given in the entire experiment.

7. Milgram carefully rehearsed the responses used by both the learner and the experimenter. The learner's protests were carefully coordinated to the "shock" being administered by the teacher. At 75 volts, the learner was instructed to express "a little grunt." At 125 volts, the learner shouted to the experimenter that the shocks were becoming painful. At 150 volts, he cried out: "Experimenter, get me out of here! I won't be in this experiment anymore! I refuse to go on!" At 180 volts, he cried out: "I can't stand the pain!" At 300 volts, he shouted in desperation that he would no longer provide answers to the memory test. At 315 volts, following

a "violent scream," he reaffirmed his prior refusal to continue participating. At 330 volts, the learner hysterically demanded, "Let me out of here! You have no right to hold me here! Let me out!" After 330 volts, the learner was not heard from again.

8. When the teacher showed any resistance to the experimenter's commands, the experimenter responded with one of the following commands:
    ▸ *Prod 1: Please continue.*
    ▸ *Prod 2: The experiment requires that you continue.*
    ▸ *Prod 3: It is absolutely essential that you continue.*
    ▸ *Prod 4: You have no other choice, you must go on.*

If the subject insisted on stopping after hearing all four verbal prods, the experimenter halted the experiment. Otherwise, the experiment was halted after the subject administered the maximum 450-volt shock.

C. MILGRAM'S SHOCKING RESULTS

1. Before conducting the experiment, Milgram asked 39 psychiatrists to predict the results. They guessed that most subjects would stop at 150 volts, that about 4 percent would go as high as 300 volts, and that just one person in 1,000 would go all the way to 450 volts.

2. The psychiatrists were wrong. Twenty-six people, or 65 percent of the 40 teachers in the first experimental version, gave the learner a 450-volt "shock."

3. Numerous replications by Milgram and other researchers produced almost identical results. It is important to note that female subjects were as likely to inflict pain on a stranger as male subjects.

D. FACTORS THAT PROMOTE OBEDIENCE

1. American society places a high value of obedience to people in positions of legitimate authority. We are taught that good children, students, and employees obey instructions and do not cause trouble. Milgram speculated that his subjects' inability "to invent a disobedient response" may be symptomatic of the pressures in our culture to conform.

2. Milgram believed that the volunteers were decisively influenced by their role of "subject" in a scientific experiment. The role of "good subject" committed them to follow the instructions of a scientist who was seen as a legitimate and trusted authority.

3. Milgram also believed that what he called the "small ignoble emotion–embarrassment" played an important role. His subjects simply couldn't bring themselves to disrupt what appeared to be a legitimate experiment.

E. FACTORS THAT REDUCE OBEDIENCE

1. Milgram conducted variations of his experiment on approximately 1,000 subjects. Taken together, his experiments comprise one of the largest research programs in the history of social psychology.

2. Milgram's additional experiments identified several conditions that reduced the willingness of his subjects to obey the experimenter:

   ▸ *When subjects were allowed to freely select the shock level, 95 percent of them did not go beyond 150 volts.*

   ▸ *When subjects observed other subjects who refused to obey the experimenter's orders, 90 percent of them refused to continue. It is very important to note that this finding corroborates Asch's discovery that subjects will stand by their convictions when they are supported by a dissenter or role model.*

Test Tip

AP Psychology test writers expect students to be thoroughly familiar with Milgram's classic study of obedience to authority. Be sure you know that 65 percent of participants administered the highest voltage shock, that subjects were least likely to deliver maximum levels of shock when they observed dissenters who refused to obey the experiment's orders, and that psychiatrists significantly underestimated the subject's level of obedience.

VII. DIFFERENTIAL TREATMENT OF GROUP MEMBERS

A. IN-GROUPS

1. An in-group is a group a person identifies with and feels that he or she belongs to.

2. The in-group bias is the tendency to judge the behavior of in-group members favorably and out-group members unfavorably.

3. The in-group bias can hinder the efforts of outsiders to join a new group. In-group members would perceive the new person as different and would not make him or her feel welcome.

B. OUT-GROUPS

1. An out-group is a group with which a person does not identify and does not feel as if he or she belongs.

2. The out-group homogeneity effect is the tendency to see members of the out-group as very similar to one another.

C. ETHNOCENTRISM

1. Ethnocentrism is the tendency to consider other cultures, customs, and values as inferior to one's own.

2. European explorers and Native Americans frequently expressed ethnocentric judgments toward each other's cultures. For example, Amerigo Vespucci insisted that the Native Americans' "manner of living is very barbarous because they do not eat at fixed times, but as often as they please."

3. It is interesting to note that both ethnocentrism and groupthink can lead to inaccurate perceptions and conclusions.

D. STEREOTYPES

1. A stereotype is a mental image of members of a group that exaggerates or oversimplifies their characteristics.

2. The famous journalist Walter Lippman coined the term "stereotype" to refer to "pictures in our heads" that accompany a category of people. Stereotypes can be either

positive or negative. For example, what mental images do you associate with football linemen and beauty queens?

E. PREJUDICE

1. Definition
   - ▸ *Prejudice is a learned prejudgment directed toward people solely because of their membership in a specific social group.*
   - ▸ *Prejudice can be both positive and negative. However, most research focuses on the causes and consequences of negative forms of prejudice.*

2. Social factors that contribute to prejudice
   - ▸ *Social divisions based upon in-groups and out-groups promote negative stereotypes and prejudice.*
   - ▸ *Inequalities between "haves," who possess wealth, power, and prestige and "have-nots," who lack social status, promote prejudice.*

3. Emotional factors that contribute to prejudice
   - ▸ *Psychological studies and historic examples both indicate that frustration intensifies prejudice. Frustration is often directed toward an innocent target known as a scapegoat. For example, Christians served as scapegoats for Rome's military defeats in the 3rd century; Jews served as scapegoats for Germany's defeat in World War I; and African Americans served as scapegoats for the South's defeat in the Civil War.*
   - ▸ *Prejudice is often directed at groups perceived as threatening important cultural values. For example, prejudice directed at gays and lesbians is incited by the belief that these groups threaten important family values.*

F. DISCRIMINATION

1. Discrimination refers to differential treatment, usually negative, directed at members of a group.
2. Remember that prejudice refers to an attitude, while discrimination refers to an action.

VIII. **INTERPERSONAL ATTRACTION**

A. DEFINITION

1. Attraction refers to positive feelings toward another person.

B. FACTORS THAT PROMOTE ATTRACTION

1. Physical attractiveness
   - ▸ *Research findings consistently indicate that physical attractiveness is one of the most important factors in explaining why people are initially attracted to others.*
   - ▸ *Research findings suggest that men place greater value on physical attractiveness and youthfulness, whereas women place greater value on maturity, financial resources, and ambition. Evolutionary psychologists explain these findings by pointing out that men associate beauty and youth with fertility while women associate financial resources and maturity with responsibility and the ability to be a good father.*
   - ▸ *According to the matching hypothesis, two members of a romantic pair are most likely to be judged by others as similar in physical attractiveness.*

2. Proximity
   - ▸ *Proximity means nearness. The principle of proximity states that people make more friends among those who live and work nearby.*
   - ▸ *Proximity promotes familiarity. Familiar people seem safe and approachable while unfamiliar people seem dangerous and threatening.*
   - ▸ *According to the mere exposure effect, repeated exposure to people or products increases the likelihood that we will be attracted to them. Advertisers and politicians use this principle when they regularly repeat the same sales and campaign ads. Repeated exposure to a negative stimulus can decrease attraction.*

3. Similarity
   - ▸ *Research findings consistently indicate that we are most likely to be attracted to people who share our interests, values, and experiences.*

> ▸ *Similarity is a major factor in promoting long-term relationships.*

C. ROMANTIC LOVE VERSUS COMPANIONATE LOVE

1. Romantic love
   - ▸ *Based upon intense feelings of attraction to another person.*
   - ▸ *Typically fades after 6 to 30 months.*
2. Companionate love
   - ▸ *Based upon strong feelings of admiration, respect, and commitment.*
   - ▸ *Strengthened by mutual sharing of decisions and the self-disclosure of intimate details about personal feelings and experiences.*

IX. AGGRESSION

A. DEFINITION

1. Aggression refers to behavior that is intended to cause harm.

B. BIOLOGICAL INFLUENCES

1. Evolutionary psychologists believe that humans are instinctively aggressive.
2. Alcohol abuse is a major factor in many forms of aggression.
3. Research studies have linked the male hormone testosterone with aggressive behavior.

C. PSYCHOSOCIAL INFLUENCES

1. According to the frustration-aggression hypothesis, frustration can ignite anger that may lead to aggression.
2. Over 1,000 studies support the connection between exposure to media violence and the likelihood that someone will behave aggressively.
3. Social rejection, minimal parental control, especially by the father, and parental models of aggression all contribute to aggressive tendencies.

D. REDUCING AGGRESSION

1. Superordinate goals
   - *Shared goals that override differences among people that cannot be achieved without a joint effort.*
   - *In the Robbers Cave Experiment (1966), Muzafer Sherif and his colleagues randomly assigned 11- and 12-year-old boys to two groups nicknamed the Eagles and the Rattlers. Posing as camp counselors, the experimenters used competitive activities to create two tightly knit in-groups. Within a short time, the Eagles and Rattlers became fierce rivals. After lectures about friendship and social events failed, Sherif used superordinate goals to reduce intergroup hostility. For example, Sherif deliberately clogged the camp's water system, thus forcing the boys to work together to fix it.*

2. Conciliatory acts
   - *Researchers have found that reciprocal conciliatory acts can begin the process of reducing tensions between hostile groups.*
   - *Diplomats often use reciprocal acts to begin peace talks. For example, negotiations between Israel and Arab nations have often started with an exchange of prisoners.*

3. Communication
   - *Communication does not guarantee a reduction in tensions.*
   - *The use of skilled third-party mediators, such as marriage counselors, labor mediators, and diplomats can help hostile parties air their differences and begin the process of establishing cooperative relations.*

Test Tip

Attraction and aggression typically are covered at the end of social psychology chapters. While students often skim over these topics, AP Psychology test writers do not. Test questions typically focus on the similarity principle as a key to explaining attraction and the frustration-aggression hypothesis as a key to explaining aggression. In addition, be sure you know that superordinate goals can be an effective way to reduce tension and conflict.

PART III:
KEY THEMES AND FACTS

Key Psychologists and Historic Figures

The AP Psychology Course Description booklet lists the names of 62 "major historical figures" and "key contributors" to the development of psychology.

These figures and contributors offered insights, designed research studies, and formulated theories that are frequently tested on the AP Psychology exam. This chapter provides a concise summary of the key contributions of each of these 62 people. See the relevant sections in Chapters 3–16 for additional information on the contributions of these key psychologists and historic figures.

I. HISTORY AND APPROACHES

1. **CHARLES DARWIN (1809–1882)**
   Darwin was a British naturalist whose controversial and groundbreaking theory of evolution had a significant influence on the early development of psychology. Darwin's theory of natural selection continues to influence the modern evolutionary perspective.

2. **WILHELM WUNDT (1832–1920).**
   Wundt is remembered as a German scientist who established the first psychology research laboratory. He pioneered a research method called introspection in which his subjects reported detailed descriptions of their own conscious mental experiences.

3. WILLIAM JAMES (1842–1910)

William James was a Harvard professor who played a key role in establishing psychology in the United States. He emphasized studying the purpose, or function, of behavior and mental experiences. According to the James-Lange theory of emotion, the experience of emotion follows a three-part sequence beginning with the perception of a stimulus. This triggers physiological arousal, which is interpreted as a specific emotion.

4. G. STANLEY HALL (1844–1924)

After studying psychology under William James, Hall established America's first psychology laboratory. He served as the first president of the American Psychological Association.

5. MARY WHITON CALKINS (1863–1930)

Like Hall, Mary Whiton Calkins studied psychology under William James. Denied a Ph.D. at Harvard, she established a psychological laboratory at Wellesley College. Calkins served as the first elected female president of the American Psychological Association.

6. MARGARET FLOY WASHBURN (1871–1939)

Margaret Floy Washburn holds the distinction of being the first American woman to be awarded a Ph.D. in psychology. She is best known for her experimental work in animal behavior.

7. SIGMUND FREUD (1856–1939)

Sigmund Freud ranks as one of the most influential thinkers of the twentieth century. He founded the psychoanalytic school of psychological thought and developed a theory of personality that emphasized the role of unconscious conflicts in determining behavior and psychological disorders. Freud placed special emphasis on how childhood experiences influenced adult personality. He believed that dreams provided a particularly important insight into unconscious motives.

8. JOHN B. WATSON (1878–1958)

John Watson was an American psychologist who departed from Wundt and the early psychologists by emphasizing the scientific study of observable behaviors rather than the study of subjective mental processes. Watson is now remembered as one of the founders of behaviorism.

II. BIOLOGICAL BASES OF BEHAVIOR

9. PAUL BROCA (1821–1880)

Paul Broca was a French physician and anatomist who discovered that the speech production center of the brain is located in an area of the lower left frontal lobe. Today, this area in the left cerebral hemisphere is referred to as Broca's area. The discovery of Broca's area revolutionized the understanding of speech production.

10. CARL WERNICKE (1848–1905)

Carl Wernicke was a German neurologist and psychiatrist who discovered that damage to an area on the left temporal lobe caused deficits in language comprehension. Today, this area in the left hemisphere is called Wernicke's area.

11. ROGER SPERRY (1913–1994)

Roger Sperry is best known for his pioneering research with split-brain patients. He demonstrated that the brain's right and left hemispheres have specialized functions.

12. MICHAEL GAZZANIGA (B. 1939)

Michael Gazzaniga continued Roger Sperry's research by advancing understanding of how the two cerebral hemispheres communicate with one another.

III. SENSATION AND PERCEPTION

13. ERNST HEINRICH WEBER (1795–1878)

Ernst Heinrich Weber was a German physician who discovered the just noticeable difference (JND) and what we now call Weber's Law. Weber's law holds that for each sense, the size of

KEY THEMES AND FACTS

the just noticeable difference will vary depending on its relation to the strength of the original stimulus.

14. GUSTAV FECHNER (1801–1887)

Gustav Fechner was a German experimental psychologist who demonstrated that mental processes can be measured.

15. DAVID HUBEL (b. 1926)

David Hubel is a Canadian neurophysiologist whose research on feature detectors helped demonstrate the presence of specialized neurons in the occipital lobe's visual cortex that have the ability to respond to specific features of an image.

16. TORSTEN WIESEL (b. 1924)

Torsten Wiesel is a Swedish neurophysiologist who collaborated with Hubel. Their joint work expanded the scientific knowledge of sensory processing and perception.

STATES OF CONSCIOUSNESS

17. ERNEST HILGARD (1904–2001)

Ernest Hilgard is renowned for his research on hypnosis and pain control. He theorized that a hypnotized person experiences a special state of dissociation or divided consciousness. As a result, the hypnotized person experiences one stream of mental activity that responds to the hypnotist's suggestions while a second stream of mental activity is also processing information that is unavailable to the consciousness of the hypnotized subject. Hilgard named this second, disassociated stream of mental activity the "hidden observer."

LEARNING

18. IVAN PAVLOV (1849–1936)

Ivan Pavlov was a world-famous Russian (and later Soviet) physiologist who devoted three decades and 532 carefully

designed experiments to studying and formulating the
principles of classical learning.

19. JOHN GARCIA (b. 1917)

John Garcia conducted pioneering research on taste
aversion. He discovered that when rats drank flavored water
before becoming nauseated from a drug that produced
gastrointestinal distress, they acquired a conditioned taste
aversion for the flavored water. Additional studies, in which
Garcia paired noise or a shock with the nausea-producing drug,
did not produce a taste aversion. Garcia's research supports the
evolutionary perspective that being biologically prepared to
quickly associate nausea with food or drink is adaptive.

20. ROBERT RESCORLA (b. 1940)

Robert Rescorla's experiments refined Pavlov's principle that
classical conditioning occurs simply because two stimuli are
closely associated in time. Rescorla's research indicated that
the conditioned stimulus must be a reliable signal that predicts
the presentations of the unconditional stimulus. To Rescorla,
classical conditioning "is not a stupid process by which the
organism willy-nilly forms associations between any two stimuli
that happen to co-occur." Instead, his research demonstrated
that "the animal behaves like a scientist, detecting causal
relationships among events and using a range of information
about those events to make the relevant inferences."

21. EDWARD L. THORNDIKE (1874–1949)

Edward L. Thorndike conducted the first systematic
investigations of animal behavior. His famous law of effect
states that responses followed by a satisfying outcome are more
likely to be repeated, while responses followed by unpleasant
outcomes are less likely to be repeated.

22. B.F. SKINNER (1904–1990)

B.F. Skinner insisted that psychologists should focus on
observable behavior that could be objectively measured
and verified. During his long career, Skinner formulated the
principles of operant conditioning. A 2002 survey ranked
Skinner as the most frequently cited psychologist of all time.

23. EDWARD TOLMAN (1898–1959)

Thorndike and Skinner believed that behavior is a complex chain of stimulus-response connections that is strengthened or "stamped in" by a rewarding consequence. Edward Tolman challenged this view by conducting a series of experiments demonstrating that rats formed a cognitive map or mental representation of a maze. They then used this prior learning to quickly find food placed at the end of the maze. Tolman concluded that learning involves the acquisition and use of knowledge rather than simply conditioned changes in outward behavior.

24. WOLFGANG KOHLER (1887–1967)

Like Tolman, Wolfgang Kohler believed that behaviorists underestimated animals' cognitive processes and abilities. In a pioneering series of experiments, Kohler suspended bananas just outside the reach of a caged chimpanzee named Sultan. Unlike Skinner's rats and pigeons, Sultan did not solve the problem through trial-and-error. Instead, he studied the situation and, in a flash of insight, used a stick to knock down the fruit. Kohler called this sudden understanding of a problem insight.

25. ALBERT BANDURA (b. 1925)

Albert Bandura is best known for his famous "Bobo doll" experiments illustrating the role of modeling in human behavior. Bandura contends that observational learning is responsible for most human behavior.

VI. COGNITION

26. GEORGE A. MILLER (b. 1920)

Although he has had a long and varied career, George A. Miller is best known for his classic paper, "The Magical Number Seven, Plus or Minus Two." Miller presented convincing evidence that the capacity of short-term memory is limited to seven items (plus or minus two) of information. It is interesting to note that memory span depends upon the category of chunks used. For example, the span is around seven for digits, six for letters, and just five for words. That helps explain why it takes so much work to learn and remember difficult SAT vocabulary words!

27. HERMANN EBBINGHAUS (1850–1909)

Hermann Ebbinghaus was a German psychologist who conducted pioneering research on forgetting. His famous forgetting curve shows a rapid loss of memories of relatively meaningless information, followed by a very gradual decline of the remaining information.

28. ELIZABETH LOFTUS (b. 1944)

Elizabeth Loftus is one of America's most influential, and most controversial, cognitive psychologists. Her extensive research on the misinformation effect demonstrated that eyewitness testimony is often unreliable and can be altered by simply giving a witness incorrect post-event information. Loftus is one of the 25 psychologists most often cited in psychology textbooks.

29. NOAM CHOMSKY (b. 1928)

Noam Chomsky is a renowned linguist who argues that young children possess an innate capacity to learn and produce speech. Chomsky notes that children in widely different cultures nonetheless progress through the same stages of language development at about the same time. He hypothesized that humans learn language because of innate speech-enabling structures called the language acquisition device or LAD.

 ## VII. MOTIVATION AND EMOTION

30. ABRAHAM MASLOW (1908–1970)

Abraham Maslow is considered the founder of the humanistic approach to psychology. While many psychologists followed Freud in studying mental disorders, Maslow focused on what constituted positive mental health. Maslow's famous hierarchy of needs begins with basic physiological and safety needs and then ascends to belonging and self-esteem. Individuals reach Maslow's top level of "self-actualization" by realizing their full potential and achieving harmony and understanding.

31. STANLEY SCHACHTER (1922–1997)

Stanley Schachter is best known for his two-factor theory of emotions. According to this theory, our emotions depend on physical arousal and a cognitive labeling of that arousal. For example, if you cry after breaking up with your boyfriend, you label your emotion as sadness. If you cry at your sister's graduation, you label your emotion as happiness.

32. HANS SELYE (1907–1982)

Hans Selye is best known for his study of stress. According to Selye's three-stage general adaptation syndrome, stress begins with an alarm reaction when people confront a stress-producing event by mobilizing internal resources such as producing adrenaline, to bring about the fight-or-flight response. If the stressor continues, the body enters a second stage of resistance characterized by heightened physiological arousal and a sudden outpouring of hormones. Long-term exposure to the stressor event eventually leads to a third stage of exhaustion that depletes the body's resources and leads to physical disorders, vulnerability to illness, and a complete collapse.

33. ALFRED KINSEY (1894–1956)

Alfred Kinsey is renowned for his pioneering research on human sexuality. Although very controversial, Kinsey's extensive research provides data that is still used as a baseline for modern research.

DEVELOPMENTAL PSYCHOLOGY

34. MARY AINSWORTH (1913–1999)

Mary Ainsworth was a developmental psychologist who devised a research procedure called the Strange Situation to observe attachment relationships between infants and their mothers.

Based upon their behavior, Ainsworth labeled the infants as either securely attached or insecurely attached. Securely attached infants tend to be well adjusted, form successful social relationships, and perform better at school. Insecurely attached infants tend to form shallow relationships, appear withdrawn, and sometimes display a strong need for affection.

35. HARRY HARLOW (1905–1981)

Harry Harlow was a developmental psychologist who conducted a famous series of experiments on rhesus monkeys. Harlow gave orphaned baby monkeys two artificial surrogate "mothers." A cloth "mother" provided no milk but offered a soft terrycloth cover. A wire "mother" provided milk but offered no contact comfort. Whenever Harlow placed a frightening stimulus into the cage, the monkeys ran to the cloth mother for protection and comfort. Harlow's research contradicted the then common belief that bodily contact would spoil children. Harlow instead concluded that the stimulation and reassurance derived from the physical touch of a parent or caregiver play a key role in developing healthy physical growth and normal socialization.

36. KONRAD LORENZ (1903–1989)

Konrad Lorenz is regarded as the founder of ethology, the comparative study of animal behavior (including humans) and their natural surroundings. Lorenz earned widespread recognition for his study of imprinting and aggression. He concluded that the mechanism inhibiting aggression works less well in humans than among other species.

37. JEAN PIAGET (1896–1980)

Jean Piaget was a Swiss psychologist whose theories of cognitive development have had a profound impact upon our understanding of how the mind develops. Unlike B.F. Skinner, who focused on environmental influences, or Sigmund Freud, who emphasized unconscious drives and conflicts, Piaget focused on the rational, perceiving child who has the capacity to make sense of the world. Piaget's stage theory describes how infants, children, and adolescents use distinctly different cognitive abilities to understand the world. Piaget identified four distinct stages of cognitive development. Each stage marks a fundamental change in how a child thinks and understands the world.

38. LEV VYGOTSKY (1896–1934)

Lev Vygotsky was a pioneering Russian psychologist. Although he died at a relatively young age, Vygotsky was a prolific author. He placed particular emphasis on how culture and social interactions with parents and other significant people influenced a child's cognitive development. According to Vygotsky, children learn their culture's habits of mind through a process he called internalization.

39. DIANA BAUMRIND (b. 1927)

Diana Baumrind is best known for her work on parenting styles. Baumrind identified three distinct parenting styles based upon "parental responsiveness" and "parental demandingness." Permissive parents set few rules, make minimal demands, and allow children to reach their own decisions. Authoritative parents set firm rules, make reasonable demands, and listen to their child's viewpoint while still insisting on responsible behavior. And finally, authoritarian parents set rigid rules, enforce strict punishments, and rarely listen to their child's viewpoint.

40. ERIK ERIKSON (1902–1994)

Erik Erikson created an influential theory of social development. According to Erikson, as we progress from infancy to old age, we enter eight psychosocial stages of development. Each stage corresponds to a physical change and takes place in a distinctive setting. This combination of physiological change and new social environments creates a psychosocial crisis that can be resolved with either a positive or a negative response. Erikson was particularly interested in the adolescent's struggle to overcome role confusion and find an identity. He coined the phrase "identity crisis" to describe how adolescents struggle to create a meaningful sense of identity.

41. LAWRENCE KOHLBERG (1927–1987)

Lawrence Kohlberg was an American psychologist who used hypothetical moral dilemmas to study moral reasoning. His influential theory of the stages of moral development is a milestone in developmental psychology.

42. CAROL GILLIGAN (b. 1936)

Carol Gilligan is best known for her critique of Kohlberg's theory of moral development. In a book entitled *In a Different Voice*, Gilligan argued that the participants in Kohlberg's basic study were all male. She contended that the scoring method Kohlberg used tended to favor a principled way of reasoning that was more common to boys. According to Gilligan, the moral concerns of women focus on caring and compassion.

IX. PERSONALITY

43. ALFRED ADLER (1870–1937)

Alfred Adler enjoyed an influential career in both Europe and the United States. Known as a Neo-Freudian, Adler pioneered the use of psychiatry in both social work and early childhood education. Adler introduced such fundamental mental-health concepts as "inferiority feeling," "life-style," "striving for superiority," and "social interest." Adler tried to help his patients "see the power of self-determination" and "command the courage" to alter their interpretation of events and life experiences.

44. CARL JUNG (1875–1961)

Carl Jung is best known as a Neo-Freudian who developed the concept of the collective unconsciousness. According to Jung, the collective unconsciousness includes shared human experiences embodied in myths and cultural archetypes, such as the wise grandfather, the innocent child, and the rebellious son. Jung's study of the collective unconscious influenced psychological thinking about humans as symbol-using beings.

45. CARL ROGERS (1902–1987)

Carl Rogers rejected Freud's pessimistic view of human nature. Instead, Rogers offered the optimistic view that people are innately good, and, thus, "positive, forward-moving, constructive, realistic, [and] trustworthy." Rogers argued that self-concept is the cornerstone of a person's personality. People whose self-concept matches their life experiences usually have high self-esteem and better mental health. Influenced by Abraham Maslow, Rogers believed that people are motivated to achieve their full potential or self-actualize.

46. PAUL COSTA (b. 1942) AND ROBERT MCCRAE (b. 1949)

Paul Costa and Robert McCrae are personality theorists best known for their work in developing the Five-Factor Model of Personality. Popularly known as the "Big Five Model," it identifies openness, conscientiousness, extroversion, agreeableness, and neuroticism as broad domains or dimensions of personality. Costa and McCrae believe that these five dimensions represent the basic structure behind all personality traits.

X. TESTING AND INDIVIDUAL DIFFERENCES

47. FRANCIS GALTON (1822–1911)

Francis Galton was a multifaceted British psychologist who had a passion for applying statistics to the variations in human abilities. Galton developed the statistical concept of correlation and was the first to demonstrate that the "normal distribution" could be applied to intelligence.

48. CHARLES SPEARMAN (1863–1945)

Charles Spearman was a British psychologist who observed that an individual's scores on various tests of intellectual performance correlated with one another. That is, people who performed well on a test of one mental ability, such as mathematical reasoning, tend to also do well on tests of verbal ability. Based upon this observation, Spearman proposed that intelligence is a single, underlying factor, which he termed general intelligence or the g factor.

49. ROBERT STERNBERG (b. 1949)

Robert Sternberg is an American psychologist best known for his triarchic theory of intelligence. The triarchic model distinguishes among analytic, creative, and practical intelligences. Sternberg believes that each of these three intelligences is learned and can therefore be developed and enhanced.

50. HOWARD GARDNER (b. 1943)

Howard Gardner is widely known for his theory of multiple intelligences. Gardner disputes Spearman's assertion that there is a single general intelligence. Instead, Gardner believes that there are a number of intelligences including linguistic, logic-mathematical, musical, spatial, bodily kinesthetic, naturalist, interpersonal, and intrapersonal.

51. ALFRED BINET (1857–1911)

Alfred Binet was a French psychologist who invented the first usable intelligence test. Binet made an important distinction between a child's mental and chronological ages.

52. LEWIS TERMAN (1877–1956)

Lewis Terman was a pioneer in educational psychology who is best known as the inventor of the Stanford-Binet IQ test. Terman computed a child's intelligence quotient or IQ by dividing mental age by chronological age and then multiplying the result by 100. Terman also conducted an influential longitudinal study of gifted children.

53. DAVID WECHSLER (1896–1981)

David Wechsler was a leading American psychologist who developed a series of widely used intelligence tests. Instead of using Terman's approach to calculate an IQ score, Wechsler determined how far a person's score deviates from a bell-shaped normal distribution of scores. Most intelligence tests now use this system.

XI. TREATMENT OF ABNORMAL BEHAVIOR

54. DOROTHEA DIX (1802–1887)

Dorothea Dix was an American reformer who documented the deplorable conditions of how states cared for their insane poor. Dix's single-minded zeal helped persuade state legislatures to create the first generation of American mental hospitals.

55. ALBERT ELLIS (1913–2007)

Albert Ellis is renowned for developing the principles and procedures of rational-emotive therapy. Ellis helped his clients dispute irrational beliefs and replace them with more rational interpretations of events. A survey of American and Canadian psychologists ranked Ellis as the second most influential psychotherapist in history. (Carl Rogers ranked first and Sigmund Freud ranked third).

56. AARON BECK (b. 1921)

Aaron Beck is widely regarded as the father of cognitive therapy. His pioneering theories are widely used to treat clinical depression.

57. MARY COVER JONES (1896–1987)

Mary Cover Jones conducted pioneering research in applying behavioral techniques to therapy. As a result, Jones is often called "the mother of behavior therapy."

58. JOSEPH WOLPE (1915–1997)

Mary Cover Jones's successful use of behavioral techniques inspired the South African psychologist Joseph Wolpe to perfect a technique for treating anxiety-producing phobias that he named systematic desensitization. Wolpe first taught his client how to maintain a state of deep relaxation. He and his client then created a hierarchy of anxiety-arousing images and situations. Wolpe and his client began with the least threatening experience and then gradually worked their way up to the top level of the anxiety-producing hierarchy.

SOCIAL PSYCHOLOGY

59. LEON FESTINGER (1919–1989)

Leon Festinger is best known for formulating the theory of cognitive dissonance. According to Festinger, cognitive dissonance is the state of psychological tension and anxiety that occurs when an individual's attitudes and behaviors are inconsistent. Although it is possible to reduce dissonance by changing either one's behavior or one's attitude, most people modify their attitudes.

60. PHILIP ZIMBARDO (b. 1933)

Philip Zimbardo is a textbook author and the developer of the popular PBS-TV series *Discovering Psychology*. Zimbardo is best known for his classic, but controversial, Stanford Prison Experiment. The experiment vividly illustrated how the process of deindividuation led to the reduction of personal responsibility and the abuse of power. Zimbardo's findings have been applied to the U.S. military abuses revealed in 2004 at Iraq's Abu Ghraib Prison.

61. SOLOMON ASCH (1907–1996)

Solomon Asch is widely recognized as one of the pioneers in developing social psychology as an academic discipline. His celebrated study of conformity provided a vivid demonstration of how individuals respond to the social pressures and expectations of others.

62. STANLEY MILGRAM (1933–1984)

Stanley Milgram's famous and controversial study of obedience to authority comprises one of the largest research programs in the history of social psychology. Milgram transformed our understanding of human nature by demonstrating that ordinary citizens were willing to obey an authority figure who instructed them to administer electric shocks to an innocent "learner." Milgram's experiment also transformed our understanding of the proper code of ethics that should be used in psychological research.

Key Trouble Spots

AP Psychology courses include a large number of difficult and easily confused terms and theories. As experienced teachers, AP Psychology test writers are very familiar with the concepts and theories that cause students the most trouble. This chapter is designed to help you by identifying and clarifying 14 of the most troublesome trouble spots. The vivid examples and carefully targeted memory tips should help you store each concept and theory in your long-term memory, so that you can easily access it during the AP Psychology exam!

1. DIFFERENTIATING BETWEEN THE INDEPENDENT VARIABLE AND THE DEPENDENT VARIABLE

▸ A significant number of multiple-choice and free-response questions are designed to test your ability to understand the difference between independent and dependent variables. An independent variable is the factor that is manipulated or controlled by the experimenter. A dependent variable is the factor that is measured by the experimenter.

▸ One way to remember how the Independent Variable works is to compare it to the IV medicine doctors inject into a patient. In the experimental method, the researcher "injects" subjects with an independent variable to see how it affects their behavior.

▸ For example, a researcher randomly assigned boys and girls to one of two groups. One group played a violent video game while the other group played a nonviolent video game. The researcher then recorded incidents of aggressive behavior for each group during a subsequent play period. In this experiment, the independent variable is the type of video game played and the dependent variable is the incidence of aggressive behavior.

2. REMEMBERING KEY PARTS OF THE BRAIN

▶ Many students feel overwhelmed by complex diagrams depicting the various parts of the brain. Relax, AP Psychology test writers will not ask you to label a diagram of the brain. However, you should know the function of key parts of the brain such as the hippocampus, the hypothalamus, and the left cerebral hemisphere.

▶ Fortunately there are good mnemonic tips that can help you remember the functions of these three often-tested parts of the brain:

1. *The "hippocampus" is involved in forming and retrieving memories. Notice, that the word hippocampus ends with the word "campus." A college campus is, of course, a place where you will soon form life-long memories that will be stored in your hippocampus.*

2. *The word "hypothalamus" also contains a good memory clue. The hypothalamus governs hunger and thirst. So, all you have to do is link the letters h and t in hypothalamus to "hunger" and "thirst." That was easy!*

3. *Finally, in order to remember that the left cerebral hemisphere specializes in language functions, link the l in "left" with the l in "language."*

3. REMEMBERING THE DIFFERENCE BETWEEN CONES AND RODS

▶ Modern AP Psychology textbooks contain impressive color diagrams depicting each part of the eye. Do not spend valuable study time trying to memorize these diagrams. Your AP Psychology exam will not ask you to label a diagram of the eye.

▶ While you will not have to label a diagram of the eye, you will be expected to understand the functions of cones and rods. Cones are responsible for color vision while rods detect shades of gray. One way to remember the difference between cones and rods is to keep in mind that both the words "cone" and "color" begin with the letter "*c*." Fans of the classic science fiction TV series *Twilight Zone*, will recall that it was produced in black and white and written by Rod Serling!

4. REMEMBERING KEY POINTS ABOUT REM SLEEP

▸ The sleep cycle and especially REM sleep generate a significant number of multiple-choice questions.

▸ Here are four key points you should remember about REM sleep:

1. *REM sleep does not begin immediately. The initial four NREM (non-rapid-eye movement) stages typically last about an hour. After completing Stage 4, the sleeper reverses back thru Stages 3 and 2 and then, instead of reentering Stage 1, the sleeper enters REM sleep.*

2. *REM sleep is highly correlated with dreams.*

3. *REM sleep is often called "paradoxical sleep" because it is simultaneously characterized by active eye movements AND the loss of muscle movement.*

4. *The amount of REM sleep changes during our life span. Infants spend about 40 percent of their sleep in REM.*

5. UNDERSTANDING NEGATIVE REINFORCEMENT

▸ Negative reinforcement can be a difficult concept to understand and apply. The key to mastering this concept is to understand the meaning of the words "negative" and "reinforcement." A reinforcement increases the probability that the behavior or response will be repeated. As used by Skinner, the word "negative" does not mean "bad" or "undesirable." Instead, Skinner used "negative" to indicate that a response is strengthened because something is subtracted or removed.

▸ It is helpful to remember that negative reinforcement typically enables you to avoid an aversive stimulus before it occurs. For example, you clean up your room to avoid the aversive stimulus of your mother's repeated scolding.

▸ Negative reinforcement can also be used to escape an existing aversive stimulus. For example, you take an aspirin to relieve a headache.

6. IDENTIFYING EXAMPLES OF FUNCTIONAL FIXEDNESS

▸ Functional fixedness is an easy concept to overlook and a hard concept to remember. AP Psychology test writers know this and have written a number of multiple-choice questions designed to test this concept.

▸ Functional fixedness is a bias that limits a person to using an object only in the way it is traditionally used. Functional fixedness thus impedes innovation by preventing people from seeing the full range of ways in which an object can be used. For example, when two children use sofa cushions to build a fort, or a young couple on a picnic uses the plastic tablecloth to protect them from a sudden downpour, they have both successfully overcome functional fixedness.

7. UNDERSTANDING THE DIFFERENCE BETWEEN THE AVAILABILITY HEURISTIC AND THE REPRESENTATIVE HEURISTIC

▸ The availability heuristic and the representative heuristic are easily confused and often tested. The availability heuristic refers to a heuristic or problem-solving strategy in which you judge the likelihood of an event based on how readily available other instances of the event are in your memory. The key word is "available." For example, 266 airline passengers were killed in the four hijacked planes on September 11, 2001. These shocking and highly-publicized terrorist attacks convinced many people to cancel their plane reservations and drive instead. These decisions were based upon the use of an availability heuristic.

▸ The representative heuristic refers to a heuristic or problem-solving strategy in which you judge the likelihood of an event by finding a comparable known event and assuming that the probabilities will be similar. The key word is "similar." For example, if you meet three students from a nearby high school and they are all very good in calculus, you will assume that their high school has an excellent math program, and that most of the other students will also be excellent in math. This judgment is based upon the use of a representative heuristic.

8. **COMPARING THE JAMES-LANGE THEORY OF EMOTION WITH THE SCHACHTER-SINGER TWO-FACTOR THEORY OF EMOTION**
    ▶ It is very easy to confuse the James-Lange theory of emotion and the Schachter-Singer two-factor theory of emotion. The following example will help illustrate the similarities and the differences between these two theories.
    ▶ Both theories begin with an emotional stimulus. For example, let's say that you have a boyfriend who is a freshman in a college located in another state. On Saturday morning your front door bell rings and, when you look out the window, you see your boyfriend holding a bouquet of flowers! Your boyfriend is the emotional stimulus. According to both theories, seeing your boyfriend triggers an emotional arousal. You raise your eyebrows, open your eyelids, drop your jaw and, at the same time, your heart "skips a beat."
    ▶ At this point, both theories are the same. First, you perceive a stimulus (the unexpected arrival of your boyfriend) and, second, the stimulus triggers physiological arousal (your heart skips a beat). According to the James-Lange theory, you then subjectively interpret your facial expressions and heart skipping a beat as surprise. According to the Schachter-Singer two-factor theory, the stimulus of seeing your boyfriend simultaneously triggers both physiological arousal and a cognitive label that makes sense of the arousal. In this example, you make cognitive sense of your boyfriend's sudden appearance by thinking, "my raised eyebrows and my heart skipping a beat are caused by surprise—I'm surprised!"
    ▶ It is important to remember that the Schachter-Singer two-factor theory of emotion includes a component *not* discussed in the James-Lange theory. And what is that component? The correct answer is cognitive labeling.

9. **REMEMBERING THE KEY CHARACTERISTICS OF THE STAGES IN PIAGET'S THEORY OF COGNITIVE DEVELOPMENT**
    ▶ Piaget's theory of cognitive development is complex, challenging, and important. While you will not have to write a detailed stage-by-stage description of

Piaget's theory, you will be expected to know the key characteristics of each of his four stages of cognitive development. The following chart is designed to help you identify and remember the key characteristics of each stage:

STAGE	KEY CHARACTERISTICS	MEMORY TIP
Sensorimotor (0–2 years)	Lacks object permanence	Link the three *Os* in *sensorimotor* with the *O* in *object permanence*.
Pre-operational (2–7 years)	Develops language skills, but cannot perform operations on concrete objects; is egocentric and animistic.	Remember, egocentric does not mean selfish.
Concrete Operational (7–11 years)	Can perform operations on concrete objects and understand conservation; but, cannot think abstractly or hypothetically.	Link the *C* in in *concrete* to the *C* in *conservation*.
Formal Operational (Age 11 and up)	Can think abstractly and hypothetically.	This is *your* stage of development!

10. MAKING SURE YOU CAN IDENTIFY EXAMPLES OF PROJECTION AND REACTION FORMATION

▸ Most AP Psychology exams contain a multiple-choice question (or two) testing your knowledge of Freud's defense mechanisms. These questions typically ask you to identify the defense mechanism that is best exemplified in an everyday situation.

▸ Students often have difficulty identifying examples of projection and reaction formation. Projection is when you transfer your own unacceptable thoughts, motives, or personal qualities to someone else. For example, you feel hostility and anger toward your AP Biology lab partner, Bryan. When Bryan text messages you that he can't make it to a study session, you hit "delete" on your cell phone, and loudly accuse Bryan of being hostile toward you.

▸ In contrast, a reaction formation is when you think or behave in a way that is the opposite of your own unacceptable thoughts and feelings. For example, although you actually dislike Bryan, you text back saying, "OK, no problem" and tell everyone that Bryan is a great lab partner who is always willing to help.

11. UNDERSTANDING THE DIFFERENCE BETWEEN RELIABILTY AND VALIDITY

▸ Reliability and validity are two key principles of test construction. They are also two of the most frequently tested concepts on the AP Psychology Exam.

▸ Reliability means that a test must produce consistent results when it is administered on repeated occasions. (Remember to link the "*r*" in "reliability" with the "*r*" in "repeat"). For example, if you take the SAT or the ACT two or more times, your scores should be similar.

▸ Validity means that a test actually measures what it was designed to measure. One way to establish the validity of a test is by demonstrating its predictive value. For example, the SAT is designed to predict academic success during a student's freshman year in college. Students who receive a high SAT score should therefore have a high grade point average (GPA) at the end of their freshman year. It is important to point out that a test can be reliable without being valid. For example, you can take the SAT several times and receive similar scores. However, your high SAT score may not be followed by a high freshman GPA.

12. REMEMBERING KEY POINTS ABOUT SCHIZOPHRENIA

▸ Schizophrenia is the most frequently tested form of abnormal behavior.

▸ Here are four key points you should remember about schizophrenia:

1. *Schizophrenia typically begins in late adolescence or early adulthood. It rarely emerges prior to adolescence or after age 45.*

2. The characteristic symptoms of schizophrenia include delusional beliefs, hallucinations, and disorganized speech and thought. Incoherent speech is often called word salad.

3. The lifetime risk of developing schizophrenia increases with genetic similarity.

4. According to the dopamine hypothesis, overactivity of certain dopamine neurons in the brain may contribute to some forms of schizophrenia. Drugs that block dopamine activity can reduce or eliminate some symptoms of schizophrenia.

13. COMPARING THE PSYCHOANALYTIC, COGNITIVE, HUMANIST, AND BEHAVIORIAL APPROACHES TO THERAPY

▸ The psychoanalytic, cognitive, humanist, and behavioral approaches offer very different ways of treating abnormal behavior. AP Psychology test writers expect you to be able to identify the focus and major techniques of each of these four approaches.

▸ The following chart is designed to help you compare and contrast the focus and techniques of these four therapeutic approaches.

APPROACH	FOCUS	MAJOR TECHNIQUES
Psychoanalytic	Unconscious conflicts that usually date back to childhood experiences	Uses free association, dream analysis, transference, and interpretation.
Cognitive	Faulty thought processes and beliefs	Rational examination of irrational beliefs
Humanist	Removing obstacles that block personal growth and potential	Empathy, unconditional positive regard, genuineness, and active listening
Behavioral	Relationships between past learning and the occurrence of a behavioral problem	Systematic desensitization and aversion therapy

14. **UNDERSTANDING THE DIFFERENCE BETWEEN THE FUNDAMENTAL ATTRIBUTION ERROR AND THE SELF-SERVING BIAS**

▶ The fundamental attribution error and the self-serving bias are both frequently tested and easily confused.

▶ The fundamental attribution error is the tendency to overemphasize dispositional factors and to underestimate situational factors when making attributions about the cause of another person's behavior. For example, you break up with your girlfriend and are late for work. Your boss makes the fundamental attribution error by interpreting your tardy arrival as yet another example of your lack of motivation and discipline. The fundamental attribution error explains how others interpret your behavior.

▶ In contrast, the self-serving bias explains how you interpret your own behavior. According to the self-serving bias, most people take credit for their success while at the same time attributing their failure to external factors beyond their control. For example, since you are aware of the situational factor that caused you to be late for work, you blame your ex-girlfriend and remind your boss of all the customers who like you.

PART IV:

TEST-TAKING STRATEGIES

Chapter 9

Strategies for the Multiple-Choice Questions

Your AP Psychology Exam will begin with a 70-minute section containing 100 multiple-choice questions. Each multiple-choice question is worth 1 point. The 100 multiple-choice questions are worth a total of 100 points, or two-thirds of the exam's 150 points. Beginning with the May 2011 administration of the APUSH exam, the College Board has changed the scoring of the multiple-choice section. The score achieved on the multiple-choice section of the exam will be based on the number of questions answered correctly. Points will no longer be deducted for incorrect answers or unanswered questions.

With this change, the "guessing penalty" is eliminated, but don't waste precious time. If you do not have any idea how to answer a question, skip it and move on. If you can eliminate two or more answers, you should use the process of elimination to make an educated guess.

A GRAND STRATEGY

The multiple-choice questions are vital to achieving a high score. Fortunately, they cover very predictable topics. The AP Psychology Course Description booklet provides a very precise outline of the 14 major content areas covered on the AP Psychology exam and the approximate percentage of the multiple-choice section devoted to each area. For example, 8–10 percent of the multiple-choice questions are devoted to social psychology. Chapter 1 provides a complete list of the 14 topical areas and the percentage of multiple-choice questions in each of these areas.

The members of the AP Psychology Development Committee have all studied the principles of good test construction. They strive to write a comprehensive test that is both reliable and valid. As a result, the 100 multiple-choice questions are very evenly distributed across each area of the Course Description outline. For example, 7–9 percent of the multiple-choice questions are devoted to the unit on learning. The test writers do not concentrate all or most of their questions on classical conditioning and short-change the other topics. Instead, they typically devote 3 questions to classical conditioning, 3 questions to operant conditioning, 1 question to biological factors, and 1 or 2 questions to social learning.

You can use this pattern of evenly distributed questions to your advantage. Your primary strategic goal is to build a winning coalition of points. You don't have to fully master each topic to score a 5 or a 4. Never forget that you only need about 110 points to score a 5 and about 90 points to score a 4. As a result, you can safely devote minimal study time to topics that you find boring or confusing. For example, although neural communication, the nervous system, and the endocrine system are important topics, they typically only generate about 4 multiple-choice questions per test. Carefully design a study strategy based on which topics you want to emphasize, which ones you want to deemphasize, and which ones you want to omit.

TYPES OF QUESTIONS

The AP Psychology multiple-choice questions are very straightforward attempts to evaluate your understanding of key concepts and theories. The questions rarely use the "EXCEPT" or "NOT" formats that confuse or trick many students. For example, there were just 3 "except" questions and 2 "not" questions out of a total of 200 multiple-choice questions on the 2007 and 2004 released exams.

The overwhelming majority of AP Psychology multiple-choice questions fall into two broad categories. About two-thirds of the questions use definitions and examples to test your knowledge of key concepts. Another 15 percent of the questions test your knowledge of key psychologists and key theories. The following two sections provide you with 10 multiple-choice questions designed to test your knowledge of key concepts and 5 multiple-choice questions designed to test your knowledge of key psychologists and theories.

PRACTICE WITH KEY CONCEPTS

1. **A preschool child says, "The clouds are angry." This child is demonstrating which of the following Piagetian concepts?**

   (A) Egocentric thinking

   (B) Object permanence

   (C) Conservation

   (D) Irreversibility

   (E) Animism

   The correct answer is E. According to Piaget, children in the preoperational stage believe that inanimate objects, such as clouds, have feelings. Answer choice A is incorrect because egocentric thinking is the inability to consider another person's point of view. Answer choice B is incorrect because object permanence is the ability to form internal images or mental representations of objects. Answer choice C is incorrect because conservation is the ability to understand that two equal quantities remain equal, even though their form or appearance is rearranged. Answer choice D is incorrect because irreversibility refers to a child's inability to mentally reverse a sequence of events or logical operations.

2. **On a test with a negatively skewed distribution, one student received the mean score, one student received the median score, and one student received the mode score. Which of these scores has the lowest percentile ranking?**

   (A) The mean

   (B) The median

   (C) The mode

   (D) All three scores are equal

   (E) It cannot be determined from the data given.

   The correct answer is A because a negatively skewed distribution contains a preponderance of scores on the high end of the scale. As a result, the mean will be lower than both the median and the mode. Answer choices B, C, D, and E are therefore all incorrect.

3. **Which of the following is the best example of the defense mechanism of repression?**

   (A) Sophia refuses to accept her doctor's suggestion that she needs to lose weight and exercise more, saying "I look fine and I don't have the time to go to a gym."

   (B) Jessica scolds her brother after being told by her parents that she is grounded for a week.

   (C) Unaware of her reputation for being stubborn and opinionated, Lily complains that her friends are inflexible and rigid.

   (D) Allison insists that she can't remember what she said that provoked a big argument with her boyfriend.

   (E) After receiving a rejection letter from one of his top college choices, John insists that he really did not want to attend the college because "it is too far from home. "

The correct answer is D. Allison demonstrates repression because she prevents anxiety-producing thoughts and painful feelings from entering consciousness. Answer choice A is incorrect because it is an example of denial. Answer choice B is incorrect because it is an example of displacement. Answer choice C is incorrect because it is an example of projection. And answer choice E is incorrect because it is an example of rationalization.

4. **Members of an investment club initially believe that they should buy 100 shares of a company they believe will report strong earnings. After additional discussion, the members of the club decide to buy 500 shares of the company's stock. This example best illustrates**

   (A) the fundamental attribution error

   (B) group polarization

    (C) social facilitation

    (D) social loafing

    (E) cognitive dissonance

The correct answer is B. Group polarization is the tendency for a group's predominant opinion to become stronger or more extreme after an issue is discussed. Answer choice A is incorrect because the fundamental attribution error is the tendency to overemphasize dispositional factors and to underestimate situational factors when making attributions about the cause of another person's behavior. Answer choice C is wrong because social facilitation is the tendency for an individual's performance to improve when simple or well-rehearsed tasks are performed in the presence of others. Answer choice D is incorrect because social loafing is the phenomenon of people making less effort to achieve a goal when they work in a group rather than when they work alone. And answer choice E is incorrect because cognitive dissonance is the state of psychological tension, anxiety, and discomfort that occurs when an individual's attitude and behavior are inconsistent.

5. **Which of the following is a brain structure that plays a crucial role in encoding memories?**

    (A) Amygdala

    (B) Corpus callosum

    (C) Hippocampus

    (D) Broca's area

    (E) Hypothalamus

The correct answer is C. The hippocampus is involved in forming and retrieving memories. Answer choice A is incorrect because the amygdala is linked to the production and regulation of emotions. Answer choice B is incorrect because the corpus callosum is a bundle of nerve fibers connecting the brain's left and right hemispheres. Answer choice D is incorrect because Broca's area is linked to speech production. Answer choice E is incorrect because the hypothalamus helps govern hunger, thirst, and other drives.

6. **After studying a long list of SAT vocabulary words, Marvin was able to recall the first and last words but had trouble remembering the words in the middle of the list. This situation is an example of**

   (A) episodic memory

   (B) proactive interference

   (C) the serial-position effect

   (D) retrograde amnesia

   (E) the tip-of-the-tongue phenomenon

   The correct answer is C. According to the serial-position effect, information at the beginning and end of a list is remembered better than material in the middle. Answer choice A is incorrect because episodic memory is a subdivision of declarative memory that stores memories of personal experiences and events. Answer choice B is incorrect because proactive interference occurs when old information interferes with recalling new information. Answer choice D is incorrect because people suffering from retrograde amnesia are unable to remember some or all of their past. And finally, answer choice E is incorrect because the tip-of-the-tongue phenomenon is a common retrieval failure that describes the feeling that, at any moment, a name or place you are trying to remember is just out of reach, but will soon pop out from the "tip of your tongue."

7. **Aileen wants to test her hypothesis that new drug X is more effective than standard drug Y in inhibiting arousal. Which of the following types of research methods is most appropriate for testing Aileen's hypothesis?**

   (A) Experimental

   (B) Case study

   (C) Longitudinal

   (D) Naturalistic observation

   (E) Survey

The correct answer is A because only the experimental method can establish a cause-and-effect relationship. All of the other answer choices are therefore incorrect.

8. **James checks the coin return every time he passes a vending machine. According to the principles of operant conditioning, his behavior is probably being maintained by which of the following schedules of reinforcement?**

    (A) Variable ratio

    (B) Fixed ratio

    (C) Fixed interval

    (D) Continuous interval

    (E) The Premack principle

The correct answer is A. In a variable ratio schedule, reinforcement is unpredictable because the ratio varies. Answer choice B is incorrect because in a fixed ratio schedule, reinforcement occurs after a predetermined set of responses. Answer choice C is incorrect because in a fixed interval schedule, reinforcement occurs after a predetermined time has elapsed. Answer choices D and E are both incorrect because they are not schedules of reinforcement.

9. **During one of her therapy sessions, Julia tells Dr. Yang, "I must be successful at everything I do or I am a complete failure." Which therapeutic method is Dr. Yang employing when she disputes Julia's statement?**

    (A) Humanistic therapy

    (B) Systematic desensitization therapy

    (C) Aversive conditioning therapy

    (D) Free association therapy

    (E) Rational emotive therapy

The correct answer is E. In rational emotive therapy, the therapist disputes a client's irrational "must" and "should" beliefs. Answer choices A, B, C, and D are incorrect because these therapies do actively dispute a client's self-defeating beliefs.

10. Which of the following is characterized by a long history of complaints about physical problems that are caused by psychological factors?

   (A) Dissociative amnesia

   (B) Somatic symptom disorder

   (C) Antisocial personality disorder

   (D) Narcissistic personality disorder

   (E) Schizophrenia

The correct answer is B. Somatic symptom disorder is characterized by physical complaints that are either extremely distressing or that prevent normal functioning. Individuals experience persistent symptoms that may or may not have a known medical cause. Answer choice A is incorrect because dissociative amnesia is characterized by a partial or total inability to recall past experiences, autobiographical information, and important information that is different from normal forgetting. Answer choice C is incorrect because antisocial personality disorder is characterized by a profound disregard for, and violation of, the rights of others. Answer choice D is incorrect because narcissistic personality disorder is characterized by a grandiose sense of self-importance, fantasies of unlimited success, and a need for excessive admiration. And finally, answer choice E is incorrect because schizophrenia is characterized by delusional beliefs, hallucinations, and disorganized speech.

KEY PSYCHOLOGISTS AND THEORIES

11. The terms "genuineness," "unconditional positive regard," and "empathetic understanding" are used to describe a type of therapy developed by which of the following psychologists?

   (A) Sigmund Freud

   (B) B.F. Skinner

(C) Albert Ellis

(D) Paul Costa

(E) Carl Rogers

The correct answer is E. These statements are all key elements of Carl Rogers's client-centered humanistic therapy. Answer choice A is incorrect because Freud is the founder of the psychoanalytic school of therapy. Answer choice B is incorrect because B.F. Skinner was a behaviorist. Answer choice C is incorrect because Albert Ellis was a cognitive therapist. And finally, answer choice D is incorrect because Paul Costa is best known for his work on the Five-Factor Model of Personality.

12. **According to Lawrence Kohlberg's theory, the process of development occurs**

   (A) in response to the type of attachment formed between a child and his or her mother

   (B) in response to parenting styles used by a child's parents

   (C) throughout life in a series of psychosocial stages

   (D) as children learn their culture's habits of mind through a process of internalization

   (E) through increasing gains in moral reasoning

The correct answer is E. Kohlberg is best known for his influential theory of the stages of moral development. Answer choice A is incorrect because it refers to Mary Ainsworth's study of the attachment between an infant and his or her mother. Answer choice B is incorrect because it refers to Diana Baumrind's research on parenting styles. Answer choice C is incorrect because it refers to Erik Erikson's theory of development. And finally, answer choice D is incorrect because it refers to Lev Vygotsky's study of how culture and social interaction influence a child's cognitive development.

13. **According to Hans Selye, which of the following is the sequence of stages in the general adaptation syndrome?**

    (A) Activating event, beliefs, consequences

    (B) Stimulus, arousal, subjective experience

    (C) Alarm, resistance, exhaustion

    (D) Openness, conscientiousness, agreeableness

    (E) Schema, assimilation, accommodation

    The correct answer is C. According to Selye, alarm, resistance, and exhaustion are the three stages of stress in the general adaptation syndrome. Answer choice A is incorrect because these are part of the "ABC" model in rational emotive therapy. Answer choice B is incorrect because these are the three stages in the James-Lange theory of emotion. Answer choice D is incorrect because these are three of the Big Five dimensions of personality. And finally, answer choice E is incorrect because these are three key concepts from Piaget's theory of cognitive development.

14. **Wilhelm Wundt is best known for**

    (A) his pioneering study of dreams

    (B) demonstrating that the brain's right and left hemispheres have specialized functions

    (C) his research on hypnosis and pain control

    (D) establishing the first psychology research laboratory

    (E) formulating the law of effect

    The correct answer is D. Wilhelm Wundt was a German psychologist who established the first psychology research laboratory. Answer choice A is incorrect because it refers to Sigmund Freud's pioneering work. Answer choice B is incorrect because it refers to Roger Sperry's pioneering work. Answer choice C is incorrect because it refers to Ernest Hilgard's pioneering work. And finally, answer choice E is incorrect because it refers to Edward Thorndike's pioneering work.

15. Elizabeth Loftus's research findings demonstrated that

- **(A)** humans learn language through an innate language acquisition device

- **(B)** gifted children lead happy and fulfilling lives

- **(C)** overcoming the inferiority complex is the primary driving force in the development of personality

- **(D)** individuals who have a strong need for achievement seek out tasks that are moderately difficult

- **(E)** eyewitness memories can be altered if a person is exposed to misleading information

The correct answer is E. Loftus is renowned for her work on the effect of misleading information. Answer choice A is incorrect because it refers to Noam Chomsky's work on language development. Answer choice B is incorrect because it refers to Lewis Terman's famous longitudinal study of gifted children. Answer choice C is incorrect because it refers to Alfred Adler's theory of personality. And finally, answer choice D is incorrect because it refers to David McClelland's research on achievement motivation.

Strategies for the Free-Response Questions

After completing the multiple-choice questions, you will receive a short break. You will then have 50 minutes to complete two free-response questions. Each question is worth 25 points for a total of 50 points.

PRACTICE MATERIALS

Practice is key to performing well on the free-response questions. Although practice will not guarantee a perfect score, it will help you to earn a high score. Both the *2007 AP Psychology Released Exam* and the *2004 AP Psychology Released Exam* include actual free-response questions and sample scored essays. Both booklets can be purchased from the College Board's online store. In addition, you should visit the AP Psychology homepage at AP Central (www.apcentral.collegeboard.org). There, you will find a full set of free-response questions and sample essays from 1999 to the present.

STRATEGIES FOR SUCCESS

Using authentic practice materials is important. Following good test-taking strategies is essential. This section will discuss 5 strategies that will help you achieve high scores on your free-response questions.

1. WATCH YOUR TIME

The free-response section is a two-part sprint. You must be focused and ready to "hit the ground running" in each section. Remember, you have only 25 minutes for each question.

If you have written an SAT or ACT essay, you should have a good sense of how much you can write in 25 minutes. Do not spend too much time on a single question or on part of a question. As you complete your answers, look at the classroom clock to make sure you are leaving enough time for each question.

2. WRITE DIRECT ANSWERS FOR FOCUSED, MULTIPART QUESTIONS

Students who prepare of the AP United States History, AP European History, and AP World History exams are taught to prepare for essay and DBQ questions that require a thesis statement, supporting evidence, and a conclusion. The AP Psychology exam uses a very different format. Its free-response questions are very focused, multi-part questions that do not require a traditional thesis-driven format. Your task is to clearly and directly answer each part of the question.

AP Psychology preparation books offer conflicting, and often confusing, advice on the best essay format. For example, do you need to write an introduction? Is it important to write a conclusion? These questions can be definitively answered by looking at two released essays from the 2007 AP Psychology exam.

The first essay on the 2007 exam presented students with a hypothetical everyday example. Ellie, "a new student at Skinner High School," attends a psychology club meeting hoping to make friends. The question asks you to illustrate four specific factors that would help Ellie's "quest for friendship" and four specific factors that would hinder Ellie's "quest for friendship."

AP Central provides an excellent sample essay for this question. Labeled "1A," the essay has a concise introductory paragraph and an excellent concluding paragraph. However, the student received no credit for these fine introductory and concluding paragraphs. Instead, the readers focused entirely on how the student defined and illustrated the 8 key concepts. The student correctly illustrated 7 of the 8 concepts and received a 7.

The student lost one point because he or she did not correctly illustrate the Schachter two-factor theory.

On pages 43–45 in the 2007 AP Psychology Released Exam booklet, you will find another scored essay on the same 2007 topic. Note that this essay does not contain either an introduction or a conclusion. Instead, this essay devotes a paragraph to each of the eight listed concepts. The author's paragraphs are short and to the point. The student defines the required concept and provides a clear illustrative example. The student correctly illustrated all 8 concepts and received an 8.

This comparison of two student essays published by the College Board provides definitive answers to the questions of style and format. Do not waste time writing an introduction and a conclusion. Instead, focus on writing clear, succinct paragraphs that define and illustrate each required part of the question.

3. BE PREPARED TO DEFINE AND ILLUSTRATE KEY CONCEPTS

The AP Psychology exam is dominated by key concepts. Free-response questions typically provide a hypothetical situation, and then ask you to define and illustrate 7–8 concepts. For example, a recent free-response question introduced test-takers to a couple learning a new routine for a dance competition. The question asked students to define and give an example of how each of the following seven concepts would affect the couple's performance: extrinsic motivation, punishment, proactive interference, endorphins, vestibular system, divergent thinking, and introversion.

While it is vital that you carefully review the key concepts defined in Chapter 2 and discussed in Chapters 3–16, memorizing definitions is not the best way to score points on free-response questions. The questions also require you to illustrate each concept. This *Crash Course* book contains a large collection of illustrative examples. Don't ignore these examples. Use them as springboards for thought. View your high school as a laboratory for studying human behavior. Try to develop the mental habit of applying the concepts you learn in your AP Psychology class to the patterns of behavior you see in school.

4. BE CALM IF YOU CAN'T ANSWER PART OF A FREE-RESPONSE QUESTION

It is very important to remember that each free-response question contains distinctive sub-parts that are independently scored. For example, the 2007 free-response question about Ellie's quest for friendship contained 8 specific concepts. Since the total question was worth 25 points, each concept was actually worth just 3.125 points. If you draw a blank on a concept, don't panic or fixate on trying to remember it. Instead, relax and tell yourself that it is only worth 3 points out of 150 points on the exam. Then move on to the next concept. Remember that you only need about 110 points to score a 5 and about 90 points to score a 4.

5. MAKE STUDYING RESEARCH METHODS A PRIORITY

The AP Psychology Development Committee works very hard to write a variety of free-response questions that cover key topics from the Course Description curriculum outline. Trying to guess which free-response questions will be asked is usually futile. However, it is true that 10 of the 18 exams from 1992 to 2009 included a free-response question devoted to research methodology. For example, go to AP Central and study the following questions: Question 2, 2000; Question 1, 2003; Question 1, 2004; Question 1, 2006; and Question 2, 2008. Studying these questions is an excellent way to review key research methods, concepts, and statistical measures.

NOTES

NOTES

NOTES

NOTES